T0146915

WHEN YOUR
VISION
SEEMS BIGGER THAN
YOU

Keep Alive God's Dream Inside of You

For unto every God's given dreams, there must be challenges, journeys, processes and trials to overcome.

PROPHET DR. MARTINS BATIRE

PhD (USA), Solicitor Non Practicing UK, LLM London, PG.Dip Legal Practice, LLB (Hons) London

Order this book online at www.trafford.com
or email orders@trafford.com

Most Trafford titles are also available at major online book retailers.

Unless otherwise indicated, all scripture quotations in this volume
are from the King James Version of the Bible.

Printed in the United States of America.

ISBN: 978-1-4907-0541-5 (sc)
ISBN: 978-1-4907-0543-9 (hc)
ISBN: 978-1-4907-0542-2 (e)

Library of Congress Control Number: 2013911633

Trafford rev. 06/26/2013

 www.trafford.com

North America & international
toll-free: 1 888 232 4444 (USA & Canada)
phone: 250 383 6864 ♦ fax: 812 355 4082

This book is dedicated to the memory of my late father, Reverend Solomon Batire, who passed into glory in February 2009. Daddy, you laid a legacy of godliness, prayer, and the fear of God for me and my siblings. It is a lasting inheritance, to which we shall ever be grateful. It is also my vow to pass this legacy on to my children and affect the world positively for Jesus Christ during my journey here on earth.

Contents

About the Author

Prophet Dr. Martins is the general overseer of Christ Miracle Evangelical Ministries International. Before meeting the Lord, he vowed never to be a follower of Christ even though both parents were ministers of the gospel.

Consequentially, his early life was riotously lived, and like the prodigal son's life, it was characterized by failures all the way. He was rusticated from a polytechnic and left two universities without completing his degree courses.

He went into the army out of rebellion and spite for his parents but went AWOL. He traveled abroad in search of a good life, using his own words, "I became a hustler in Taiwan, China, Israel, and Hong Kong." However, God's covenant with his parents regarding him was intact.

He later embarked on a journey to the United Kingdom where he claimed asylum. And from the point of entry, he was placed in detention centres and, later, in immigration prison for a total period of twenty-two months. While in prison, he was fed up of life, and he attempted suicide four times. But God had a plan for his life.

Still being suicidal, the Lord used the prison chaplain to supply him with the book titled *From Prison to Praise*. At the end of it all, Prophet Dr. Martins finally submitted to Christ and accepted him as his Saviour and his Lord. The Lord used the prison, which he called wilderness, to break him, make him, and fill him so that he can use him in a time as now.

Out of seventy-five thousand applicants that applied to the UK government in 1998, Prophet Dr. Martins was one of five persons that were granted full refugee status. He was divinely orchestrated to meet his wife, Pastor Helen. In 2001, through him, the Lord pioneered his church in the United Kingdom.

Prophet Dr. Martins, a prophetic teacher of the word, is a Spirit-filled preacher of the gospel, who always ministers from the practical viewpoint of life experiences. God's vision in his hand has affected lives in a positive way with testimonies and tangible miracles following.

Academic Footnote

Prophet Dr. Martins Batire is a PhD holder of philosophy of pastoral ministry from Newburgh Theological Seminary, Ohio, United States. He also obtained a master's degree in law from Westminster University, London; a postgraduate diploma in legal practice from a law school in London; and a bachelor's degree in law from Westminster University, London.

Personal Summary

Prophet Dr. Martins Batire, a qualified but Non Practicing solicitor of the Senior Courts of England and Wales, is married to Pastor Helen, also a graduate of economics and accountancy. They have two children in their marriage, namely, Martins Jr. and Princess.

Prophet Dr. Martins is a prophet with an apostolic mandate that will storm the world's stage by surprise. A day before the July 2005 bomb attempt in London, the Lord revealed through him to a praying audience the evil plan of the enemy for the following day. God has spoken several prophetic words through him into people's lives, which have not fallen to the ground. He is a man raised by God with a calling of Abraham to raise sons (disciples) and to birth and lead a movement for the Lord in this end-time.

Prophet Dr. Martins Batire, popularly referred to as the Coach, is an expository preacher of the Bible and a worshipper that encourages and motivates sons of God to worship in spirit and in truth.

Preaching Engagement

As a prophet, an apostle, and a preacher of the gospel, Prophet Dr. Martins Batire has traveled to the USA, Dubai, Ireland, Africa, and within the United Kingdom, preaching the gospel of Christ; and several miracles and testimonies confirm his mandate. If you are led by the Lord to invite Prophet Dr. Martins Batire to minister in your church events, conferences, and crusades, contact us at invite@csbci.org.uk.

Preface

This book is dedicated to the Holy Spirit, my comforter, teacher, the spirit of truth that has inspired me to write for generations even yet unborn so that they can be guided into all godly knowledge and truth and, therefore, become mature sons of God.

It has been said that the richest place on earth is the graveyard because, there, you will find many dreams that were never achieved, all because the dream carriers failed to understand the processes that must first be endured; they equally failed to be acquitted with God, the giver of dreams and the fulfiller of dreams.

Therefore, this book has been written, by the inspiration of the Holy Spirit, to encourage everyone who acknowledges that God-given dream is embedded inside of them. Equally, this book is aimed at equipping such people with the understanding of how to ensure its accomplishment. The concept of the book is based on the story of Joseph in the book of Genesis, a young man that pursued his dream through painful processes but, through God, was able to accomplish them even in a strange land—Egypt, where he entered as a slave, an immigrant, and later, jailed.

A word of encouragement to all readers of this book—please ensure that you do not read this treasure book just as you read a novel, but ensure that you engage your whole being; get your Bible by your side and take time to study all the scriptures' references mentioned therein so that, by so doing, you are well informed of God and, hence, receive his revelation that will empower you to become sons that, indeed, do exploits for the kingdom through the accomplishment of God-given dreams that were embedded inside of you.

In conclusion, please always remember that you are a spirit being, you live in the body, and you have a soul. So ensure that your spirit being is growing and well nourished even as you look after your body and soul. Shalom. Shalom.

Prophet Dr. Martins Batire, PhD

Acknowledgement

In general, my sincere appreciation goes to everyone that was there for me during the writing of this book, to all my fellow co-laborers in the vineyard of the Lord, both within and outside of Christ Shalom Bible Center, Christ Miracle Evangelical Ministries International. May the Lord continue to bless you all.

In particular, I must thank members of my family for their valuable support, without which completing this book would have been difficult. First on the list is my mother, Prophetess Remi Batire, who taught me how to prevail in prayer until the answer came. Second is my wonderful wife, Pastor Mrs. Helen Batire, who has been a very reliable shoulder to rest and cry on; you are indeed my and God's *choice*, God's choice for my life. Third are my beautiful son and daughter, Martins Jr. and Princess, the beauties of my world—I love you all.

My gratitude also goes to all my church family in Christ Shalom Bible Center (CMEMI); I am very proud to belong to the "Shalomite" family, and I, indeed, appreciate your words of encouragement.

Most importantly, I must appreciate my heavenly Father, the Most High God; my Lord and Saviour, my best friend and brother, the Lord Jesus Christ. I also appreciate my comforter and teacher, the Holy Spirit, who has made this book possible. I vowed to serve you unto eternity.

CHAPTER 1

God's Dreamer Boy — Joseph

The story of the dreamer boy, also known as Joseph, started in the book of Genesis 30: 22-25, with some difficult moments for his mother, Rachel, for whatever reason best known to God.

> And God remembered Rachel and God hearkened to her, and opened her womb. And she conceived, and bares a son; and said God hath taken away my reproach: and she called his name Joseph; and said, The Lord shall add to me another son. (Genesis 30:22-24)

I know some scholar of the Bible will suggest that this was due to the fact that Leah was hated, but when you check on Genesis 29:31, the Bible recorded that when God saw Leah was hated, God opened her womb, but Rachel was barren. The Bible did not say that God made Rachel barren.

Coming back to our point, Rachel went through a very difficult period of barrenness; even the Bible recognised that, for real, she was barren. It must have been very painful, indeed, to be married to a husband whom she truly and sincerely loved but was unable to give him even a child. It became more depressing when her blood sister, married to her husband, produced babies year in, year out.

Given the rivalry between the two women, one can imagine the silent pain of Rachel, particularly when she sent her stepchildren on errands or disciplined them whenever they were wrong. The reaction of Leah towards her was hostile and unimaginable, but given that she had the spirit of a dreamer inside of her, she stayed put in her marriage with godly patience and perseverance.

May I, at this point, encourage all would-be mothers, who have been in marriage for a while, praying for a fruit of the womb; I have got news for you: Continue to trust God and wait for him patiently; he is a faithful God. The Bible recorded in Genesis 30:22 that God remembered Rachel, hearkened to her, and opened her womb. As a prophet of God unto nations and Abraham of this generation, I declare that, as you are reading this treasure book, may your womb begin to open in Jesus Christ's name, may the heavenly Father remember you right now in Jesus Christ's name, and may he hearken unto your prayers and give you a Joseph.

I said earlier on that Rachel was a dreamer; yes, despite several years of barrenness, she continued to hope for the day when she too will celebrate with her baby. You will also note this spirit of a dreamer in Rachel even after giving birth to Joseph. The Bible says in Genesis 30:24 that she named Joseph by his name, and the meaning of *Joseph* is "the Lord shall add to me another son."

Indeed, she was a dreamer with a solid reliance on God, and not too long, God gave her Benjamin; the dream of another son was, indeed, fulfilled.

It was no surprise, therefore, that Joseph began to dream of great things while he was still a little boy. Joseph had it in his DNA; it was an inheritance from his mother. It may also be concluded that while Joseph was growing up, the mother taught him the fear of God, which was the beginning of wisdom, and she must have taught him how to meditate in the Word of God and pray to the God of Abraham. I, therefore, submit to you that there is no way that such a boy will have grown up into something else than a God-dreamer, a man that will grow to carry the dream of God for his generation. Just as Joel 2:28 says, when the Holy Spirit is poured on us, then God's dreams and visions will certainly follow, and that is notwithstanding of age.

Even in our days, God is looking for another Holy Ghost-raised Joseph that has been trained by a Rachel in the ways and in the Word of God and also exposed to prayer from their childhood. God wants to pour his dreams into such godly children so that they can become achievers and rescuers of their generation.

Questions to all parents that read this book, in particular, those with little kids or those of you that are still in the waiting room of God: Will you fail God in the lives of your children? How are you raising them up—with the demonic culture in your society, through the ungodly images on your television screen? Or will you raise them up in the fear of God, will you teach them how to pray and trust God in everything, and will you teach them to make the word of God their friend?

I encourage you all to become another Rachel and another Lois and Eunice, who equally raised another God-dreamer, called Bishop Timothy.

In 2 Timothy 1:5, Paul acknowledged that the genuine faith seen in Timothy first dwelt in Lois, his grandmother, and also in Eunice, his mother. This aligned with the case of Joseph, whose mother was also a dreamer. An adage says that you cannot give what you do not have. In the case of Timothy, both his mother and his grandmother had genuine faith; it ran in the family bloodline. Notwithstanding the two mothers' busy schedules as mother, grandmother, wives, and possibly, businesswomen, they still found time to pass on to Timothy the *genuine faith*.

They passed it on, not only in their spoken words, but also equally in their day-to-day lives, in their actions and reactions to others, and in the way they took God seriously. It must be said that genuine faith is the source of all God-given dreams, for the Bible says in the book of Hebrews 11:6 and in Hebrews 11:1 that

> Now faith is the substance of things hoped for, the evidence of things not seen. (Hebrew 11:1)

Every God-dreamer must have the "now faith" that, once possessed, becomes a substance of things hoped for, a God-given dream that—once given by God and acted on by faith by the receiver, in God's own appointed time and season—must come to pass.

It could also be said that these two women, Timothy's mother and grandmother, had raised him not only in God's genuine faith but also in the study of the Holy Scripture, and it was this early study of the Word of God, carried on in the home, that grounded the soul of young Timothy and prepared him to become, in due course, an apostle of the church and the bishop of Ephesus, a dream come true. The whole church, for the past two thousand years, owes to these two women an immense and unpayable debt of gratitude.

When, as a child, Timothy was taught the grammar of Holy Scripture, what did he learn from Lois and Eunice? Many things, to be sure, but let us consider three benefits to be ascribed to that early instruction in God's word.

First, Timothy learned to take possession of his heart, the rich and varied narratives that enabled him to make sense of his heart. Placing his young soul under the authoritative guidance of the Word of God, Timothy also learned and discovered who he was, his place in this world, what God expected of him, and what he himself could expect, both during his life and at the end of it; a God-dreamer was shaped in Timothy by a grandmother and a godly mother.

The stories of the Bible—but more especially, the central story assimilated in the context of his family—gave shape to Timothy's moral imagination, conferring on his conscience a narrative, moral sense. These biblical stories gave imaginative organisation to his mind. He was enabled to inform and fashion his personal life based on the Word of God. From the scripture meditation, learned especially in the setting of his home, Timothy was educated in the habits of the heart. He was in the full, rich sense of that word—indoctrinated, sacred doctrine being placed in the heart and mind—giving formation to his character. Timothy learned, from the inside, the Bible's perspective on the world. He slowly became versed in the spirit of the Word of God that would enable him to organize his own heart, giving structure to his thoughts and feelings in line with the scriptures.

In conclusion on this chapter, we must all realize that we are all making the future. Today, we have teenagers creating menace in our world, all because parents, when the children were in their younger ages, failed to train them in the way of the Lord. The Bible says in Proverbs 22:6 that we should "train up a child in the way he should go: and when he is old, he will not depart from it." It is just the way those children have been trained by their parents when they were children that has now become a permanent problem to our society. It is our prayer that God of heaven will reach out to those lost children, but please, while you are still able to mold them, even right now at this tender age, please be a Rachel, create another Joseph—a God-dreamer that will bring solution to our world's problems. May the good Lord help us all.

CHAPTER 2

God's Dreamer and Righteous Living

To everyone that has within them God's deposited dreams; you must live a righteous life. You must be separated from all pollutions that surround us. Why? Because you are a carrier of God's dream. In the book of 2 Corinthians 6:17, we are required to come out from among them and be separate, and we are required not to touch the unclean thing, and there is a promise from God that he will receive us.

In the above passage, God is speaking to carriers of his dreams. He is mandating them to come out from among them. This was the same message that God gave to Abraham in Genesis chapter 12:1, wherein he was required to get out of his known country, kindred, and his father's house. Why, because Abraham was God's dream carrier.

Just like he did with Father Abraham, God is calling every dream carrier of his to get out of their familiar country—meaning, a call unto salvation. Such are required to renounce patriotism to the devil's nationality, which signifies the world (cosmos) and its satanic agendas (John 15:18-19, John 17:14-19).

In the journey unto righteousness for Abraham, God stripped him of his kindred (relatives)—this signifies the flesh, our old lives, and ungodly way of doing things, fleshly thinking, and fearful and doubtful natures (Ephesians 4:17-29).

Lastly, God asked Abraham to vacate his father's house and move by faith into the unknown future but with a known and certain God. The request for Abraham to vacate his father's house signifies departure from household habits, sins, iniquities, and transgressions (Psalms 51:2-5). This same call of living a life of righteousness is required of anyone today who is a carrier of God's dream.

So in Genesis chapter 37:1, it was mentioned that Joseph, with his family, resided in a strange land, but he refused to copy the behaviour of the strange land. He made a conscious decision not to compromise his godly and Christian beliefs. He held on to the God of Abraham, Isaac, and Jacob. He refused to allow peer pressure from his age-mate to coerce him into breaching the law of God. As a result of his stand, he was in the minority, he lost friends, and he was persecuted, ridiculed, and reproached; but he stood with righteousness, the one key factor that kept the dream of God growing and alive inside of Joseph.

As if being attacked from outside was not enough, even his own brothers—who, by now, have corrupted themselves—were now operating under the spirit of the land, a spirit that Ephesians chapter 2:2 referred to as the spirit of the air that now operated in the heart of the disobedient to God. It may amaze you to know that Judah, a symbol of praise and worship, was among Joseph's brothers that were corrupted by the spirit of the land of Canaan. Know that your involvement in church activities, your titles, and your responsibilities to your church are not enough to keep the dream of God alive in you; you must ensure, through the help of the Holy Spirit that you allow the fruit of righteousness to grow and further develop into full maturity inside of you.

The Bible recorded in Genesis 37:2 that at the age of seventeen, Joseph was already set and solid in the ways of the God of heaven because he was God's dream carrier. However, as God's dream carrier with solid establishment in righteousness, he could not condole and tolerate the sinful behaviour of his brothers. Owning to the level of righteousness in Joseph, his spirit became agitated and unsettled as a result of the evil behaviour of his brethren, and the Bible says in Genesis 37:2 that he reported them to his father. Joseph was in obedience to the word of God in the book of Ephesians 5:11, wherein it was instructed by God that we should not have fellowship with the unfruitful works of darkness but rather reprove them.

It is rather unfortunate in our days today that many would-be God's dream carriers have failed to be and act like Joseph in his days. While in their places of work, they enjoy all the foolish jesting and ungodly jokes that their colleagues and workmates engage in, and they laugh and giggle whenever sinful words are uttered. No wonder they cannot be recognised and identified in their offices as God's dream carriers.

It is appalling and disgraceful to the heavenly watcher that some Christians are even the ones that indulge in the worldly and sinful behaviours seen among unbelievers. They lie, they burst into wrath, and they fornicate and indulge in sexual, filthy, and unholy behaviour. They keep boyfriends and girlfriends and commit sexual acts with them. They cohabit with partners that they are not married to; some even attend nightclubs, looking for satisfaction where there is none.

They have babies out of wedlock, and some even commit abortions, therefore, murdering lives that could have been alive today. Oh, some are wife beaters, smokers, and alcohol drinkers, and do not be surprised that come the following Sunday, they shall be the first to arrive in church. They are members of choirs, ushers, even teachers, pastors, evangelists, church committee members, bishops, apostles, and prophets. They carry titles and are very eager to put up acts; they only manage to deceive man, but they cannot deceive God, the dream giver.

Just like Joseph, true God's dream carriers are not only expected by God to distance themselves from the spirit of the land and the disobedient children but also required to expose them. This means that they are required to expose the darkness created by the spirit of the land and the acts of the disobedient people by allowing their light to extremely shine before these men (Matthew 5:16), and as a result of the light of God shining through them, their evil report has been exposed, and peradventure, God willing, some of them may be saved by God and be translated into the marvelous light of Christ.

The consequences of God's dream carrier taking sides with righteousness are mixed in nature. There are advantages and disadvantages to making God-informed decision through the Holy Spirit, enabling power to stand for righteousness. First, we read in Genesis 37:3 that Joseph's father loved him more than all his children. Verse 3 says that Jacob loved Joseph because he was the son of his old age. Although his father, Jacob, was about ninety-one years old when Joseph was born, he was not the last born.

Benjamin was born nine years after Joseph, and there was no such record of equal love and treatment. Hence, the phrase in verse 3 must have referred to a son that was especially devoted to the care of Jacob in his old age. Perhaps, after the death of Rachel, Joseph became his father's special helper in supplying his wants and being an agent between him and his other brothers. I also submit that Jacob was so impressed with Joseph's godly and righteous living and the fact that he chose not to compromise his Christian beliefs even though his brethren had done so.

Consequently, this positioned Joseph in a privileged position that enhanced him to enjoy his father's blessings—one of which was a blessing of a coat of many colours, which truly signified him as a beloved son of Jacob. The coat of many colours worn by Joseph confirmed the mark of honour and his rank among his brethren as this can only be worn by the chief and heir; hence, Joseph inherited the birthright of the firstborn even though by birth he was second to the last.

> *Now the sons of Reuben the firstborn of Israel, (for*
> *he was the firstborn; but forasmuch as he defiled his*
> *father's bed, his birthright was given unto the sons of*

Joseph the son of Israel: and the genealogy is not to be reckoned after the birthright. For Judah prevailed above his brethren, and of him came the chief ruler; but the birthright was Joseph's. (1 Chronicles 5:1-2)

The garment was of many colours, not pieces, making it, therefore, a priestly and royal garment and possibly with fine and beautiful needlework of various coloured threads (cross-reference Exodus 28:2-14, Exodus 39:1-7, 2 Samuel 13:18, and Psalms 45:14).

Just like Joseph that received a cloth of many colours, so also does every one of God's dream carrier that resolved to work in God's kind of righteousness; they are clothed with the cloth of salvation as a priest of God first (2 Chronicles 6:41), have been saved by Christ's bloodshed on the cross, and are being saved daily from the devil's temptation to sin and fall from God's grace.

According to Job 29:14 and Psalms 132:9 and16, for such God's dream carrier that embraces God's kind of righteousness, their righteousness becomes their God-given royal cloths that enable them to make a right judgment on every occasion; their right judgment also becomes their royal robe.

According to Isaiah 32:17, such God's dream carriers that embraced God's kind of righteousness shall be clothed with God's peace, quietness, and assurance forever. Psalms 85:10 confirmed that God's mercy and God's truth that establishes shall meet on them as righteousness and peace kiss (knitted like a threaded robe) together. Psalms 5:12 states that they are surrounded with goodwill, pleasure, and favour. Philippians 3:9 says that such will have a right standing with God. Revelation 1:6 and chapter 5:10 say that such God's dream carriers are made a kingdom and priests to his God and Father; they are also built like living stones into a spiritual house to be a holy priesthood, offering spiritual sacrifices acceptable to God through Jesus Christ (1 Peter 2:5). And finally, in 1 Peter 2:9, the Bible confirms the royal and priesthood status of God as conferred on every God's dream carrier.

> *But you are a chosen people, a royal priesthood, a holy nation, a people belonging to God, that you may declare the praises of him who called you out of darkness into his wonderful light. (1 Peter 2:9)*

If only you can resolve today to abide in God's righteousness through the enabling power of the Holy Spirit, your loving and heavenly Father—who is equally the father of our Lord Jesus Christ, the dream giver—will robe you with your coat of many colours just as Jacob did unto Joseph.

CHAPTER 3

Opposition Begins at Home

And a man's foes shall be *they of his own household.*

—Matthew 10:36

In the light of the Word of God that was stated above, every God's dream carrier must understand that upon your resolution to walk and live your daily life in God's righteousness, you will activate the blessing of God upon your life, and consequently, this, in many cases, will expose you to a strong opposition, even from your household.

This was the case with Joseph, a righteous man that enjoyed the love of his father, and the Bible recorded in the book of Genesis chapter 37:4 that when his brothers saw that their father loved him more than all his brothers, they hated him and could not speak peaceably unto him.

The Bible said that the brothers saw that their father loved him. So also it is for every God's dream carrier that chooses to live a righteous life; when God begins to shower his love upon you, it will be undeniably visible for everyone to see (Proverbs 21:13).

The Bible recorded in the book of Luke 3:22, Mark 1:11 and Matthew 3:17 regarding Jesus Christ—the righteous one, that God loved him so much to the extent of breaking all principles of human existence. God had to open heaven and speak directly to the inhabitants of the earth that Jesus Christ was his beloved Son.

No wonder the book of 2 Peter 1:17 confirmed that Jesus Christ received honour and glory from God the Father when God spoke to him from the excellent glory that he was God's beloved Son, in whom God was well pleased. I submit to you that God's voice was heard on that day, not only by Jesus Christ, but also by everyone present there. That included the Pharisees, Sadducees, scribes, and other Jews that later put Jesus Christ to death for claiming to be the Son of God.

Just like Joseph's brothers were to Joseph, fellow nationals and their leaders hated Jesus Christ and ensured that he was crucified; even his brothers envied him and even reproached him. Why? Because he was loved by God.

There is also a lesson that can be learnt from the open love showered by Jacob on his son Joseph. The Bible said that Joseph's brothers hated him because their father loved him. It was unwise of Jacob to show open favoritism or prefer a child above other children of the family. In many sad cases, this has led to division within such homes. It grows so bad to the extent that those children end up with abhorring grudges against their parents.

I heard of a case wherein a parent treated their daughter like a slave while growing up with them. Out of three children, this girl worked like a slave while the other kids enjoyed life like spoiled children. Whenever there was a dispute between the girl and the other children, the parents always sided against this girl, even in cases where she was clearly in the right. Her parents always showered gifts on the other children while ignoring their daughter. Consequently, they all grew up into adults, and up till today, there is rivalry and unhealthy relationship between them, which only God can resolve.

Not far away is my own childhood season, which I can describe as totally unhealthy, but I thank God that, today, he has healed me of all past pains. I grew up in a family of seven—my parents, my five siblings, and myself. Throughout my teenage season, my mother was a loving mother that loved all her children equally (maybe she had her favorite, but she never showed this) while my late father made it so obvious that he loved my siblings more than me. I grew up feeling resentful of my father (who, by the way, was a pastor in a Pentecostal church).

This I later transferred to God; I hated church, and I refused to follow my parents to church or even live a life expected of a pastor's son. This caused a rivalry between my siblings and me. I could not stand them because I felt cheated; being the first son and firstborn of the family, I was angry that my position had been taken by them. It is the grace of God today that makes me what I am now. It was his grace that saved me and healed the rivalry that existed between my family and me. Suffice it to add that my father and I made amends before his passing into glory, and we became best of friends.

I, therefore, admonish all parents to ensure that you do not show favoritism while raising up your children; do not destroy your future. And to other parents who have been victims of this situation or whose children are now grown into adults and the damage has been done in the past, there is nothing God cannot do; pray to God for the healing of the wounds and the restoration of peace to your entire family.

The opposition that Joseph experienced was from his brothers within his household, just because his father showered love on him. This situation may equally arise in the lives of God's dream carriers that resolve to walk in righteousness; you must not be unaware of household enemies. The devil may raise opposition, attack, and trials through your natural parents, brothers, sisters, and other family members. Watch out, be vigilant, and pray always; do not be discouraged and, therefore, seized from walking in righteousness, but rather, know and understand that you are on the right track and you are carrying God's dream.

Your family circle that the devil may use to oppose you may be in your church family. It is generally accepted by all that once you are saved and belong to God's church, it becomes your family too. The church family circle was meant by God to bring perfection of the saints, to bring edification of the body of Christ, and to bring all into the unity of the faith and of the knowledge of the Son of God unto a perfect man. God intended the church family to bring us all unto the measure of the stature of the fullness of Christ, to make us all fitly joined together, and to provide every joint supply (Ephesians 4:11-13).

What a great church family we shall all enjoy if all our Christian churches all around the globe fall within the description above. However, it is very sad to note and say that this is not the case in most churches. Hence, your family church may be an instrument in the hand of the devil to raise opposition against you, all because the Lord has showered his love upon you. The devil may engage your pastor to bring the opposition.

Listen to me—you are God's dream carrier; either you are serving as a commission officer (minister, deacon, elder, etc.) or you are serving as an ordained officer of the church in the capacity of a pastor, evangelist, teacher (and any of the fivefold ministries). Be prepared for an opposition, even from your leading and senior pastor, bishop, or apostle, who cannot handle God's blessings, spiritual gifts, and financial blessings over your life. (Some are unable to do so because of insecurity and lack of self-confidence in God. They have moved away from the part of righteousness; hence, they have lost or aborted the dream of God inside of them.)

You must not be distracted because that is what the devil wants to achieve. Always trust in God that started a good work in you that is able to complete it, even until the coming of the Lord Jesus Christ. Call into mind the case study of Joseph, who, in spite of the internal opposition, refused to be deterred; he trusted God, the giver of good dreams, he was humble enough to respect them, and he was holy enough to pray for those that despitefully used him but bold enough to stand confident and peaceful enough to remain calm and in control.

You must also remember the case of David, another one of God's dream carrier, who received severe opposition from

King Saul; understand this—that God's perfect plan was to use King Saul (a man possessed with an evil spirit) to mentor and prepare David for the future duties of a king. So also are you; all opposition—whether from your natural family, from your church family, or from your husband, wife, or anywhere—God has permitted them to develop in you godly characters, such as patience, and it's a must that patience has her perfect work inside of you, "that ye may be perfect and entire, wanting nothing" (James 1:4).

So whenever you experience opposition and hatred from people you expect to love you, care for you, and celebrate you, ensure that their oppositions are due to the grace, the love, the gift, and the blessing of God in your life. If it is, just stay calm in prayer; stay close to the Word of God; listen to the heartbeat of God through the Holy Spirit's guidance; continue to humble yourself under the mighty hand of God, who will exalt you in his due season; and continue to pray for those that despitefully use you and see how God will continue to bless you the more, even in the presence of the enemy.

Suffice it to say, though, that if you are experiencing what you call opposition and pressure from within your natural family—but more importantly, your church family—and it is because of your disobedience, rebellious behaviour to authorities, and lifestyles of iniquity and sin, you must repent, ask God for forgiveness, and amend your wrongs. May the Lord help us all.

CHAPTER 4

Rest in God and Dream On

And Joseph dreamed a dream, and he told it his brethren:
and they hated him yet the more. And he said unto them,
Hear, I pray you, this dream which I have dreamed: For,
behold, we were binding sheaves in the field, and, lo, my
sheaf arose, and also stood upright; and, behold, your
sheaves stood round about, and made obeisance to my
sheaf. And his brethren said to him, Shalt thou indeed
reign over us? or shalt thou indeed have dominion over
us? And they hated him yet the more for his dreams, and
for his words. And he dreamed yet another dream, and
told it his brethren, and said, Behold, I have dreamed a
dream more; and, behold, the sun and the moon and the
eleven stars made obeisance to me. And he told it to his
father, and to his brethren: and his father rebuked him,
and said unto him, what is this dream that thou hast
dreamed? Shall I and thy mother and thy brethren indeed
come to bow down ourselves to thee to the earth? And his
brethren envied him; but his father observed the saying.

—Genesis 37:5-11

It had been established in the life of Joseph that, indeed, he was a righteous man, a man that had been taught and brought up in the way of God of Abraham, and a man that took a stand against the evil behaviour of his time and society. Hence, it is understandable and expected that God will conceive in him godly dreams, spelling out his future plans through Joseph. So also is the case with every righteous men and women who have no self-righteousness, as apostle Paul put it, but who have, through the Holy Spirit, induced belief in God and responded in total obedience to God and his Word and obtained God's righteousness just as Father Abraham did (Romans 4:3, Galatians 3:6).

When you are declared righteous by God of righteousness, age is irrelevant to the level of achievement, both spiritual and physical, that God will birth through you. The book of Joel 2:28 established that it was the sole right of old men and women to have dreams. If I must analyse this further, my submission will be thus: until you have grown up to an old age, you are not entitled to have God's kind of dream that comes as a result of the outpouring of the Holy Spirit. However, Joseph and so many people in his class (youths) broke this record, and even in their teenage age, they were put down in history as God's dream carriers.

> And it shall come to pass afterward, that I will pour out
> my spirit upon all flesh; . . . Your old men shall dream
> dreams. (Joel 2:28)

The question, therefore, is, why has the book of Joel restricted God's kind of dreams to just the class of older men. The reason is not far-fetched. It should be agreed upon without any contention that older men are fathers; it should also be agreed upon without any contention that some men will easily pass the test of being called older men. With the above in view, Apostle John, in the book of 1 John 2:13 provided the clue. Apostle John in his epistle confirmed the primary stage of fatherhood (older men) in the realm of the spirit as a person that had known him that is from the beginning. Apostle John went further to confirm the secondary stage of fatherhood (older men) as anyone that had overcome the wicked one.

Hence, there are two classes of persons and two classes of responsibility. First class of person is the one that is from the beginning, and the second class is the wicked one. The responsibilities or duties are to know him that is from the beginning and overcome the wicked one. With no dispute in any Christian mind, we should all agree that the one that is from the beginning is God the Father, the Son, and the Holy Spirit. The book of John 1:1-5, Hebrews 5:8-9, Revelation 1: 17-18 and 2:8, Colossians 1:16, John 5:17-18, John 8:58, John 10:30-33, John 14:9-11, and Revelation 22:13 confirm this. Also, there should be no dispute that the wicked one is Satan (the devil) and his emissaries.

To Know Him that Is From the Beginning

To really understand what qualified the likes of Joseph to become God's dream carrier, one needs to understand the meaning of *to know* as used by Apostle John in describing the fatherhood status, and a better definition is in no other place than in the Hebrew language. The Hebrew meaning of *to know* is "Yada." Actually, the word is versatile and has several meanings, depending on the context. Let's take a look at a few examples:

Yada: Sharing Love

The first example of *Yada* can be found in the book of Genesis. The Bible says that

> Adam knew [Yada] his wife Eve and she conceived and bore Cain . . . Cain knew [Yada] his wife and she conceived and bore Enoch . . . Adam knew [Yada] his wife again, and she bore a son and named him Seth. (Genesis 4:1, 17, 25).

Here, we see a very intimate kind of knowledge and relationship. In other words, *Yada* is dedicating ourselves to the Almighty God so that we can engage God with our love and affection. It is the act of intimate relationship with God by the leading of his Spirit. In the light of this understanding, a father (older man) is someone (irrespective of their earthly age) that has got a deep and intimate relationship with God through his Son, Jesus Christ, and by the help of the Holy Spirit. Surely, Joseph—irrespective of his age, naturally speaking—was qualified to be called an older man (a father) because he had a deep relationship and intimacy with God that was from the beginning.

Yada: Acting Justly

Another occurrence of *Yada* can be found in the book of Proverbs; therein, we see an incredible blending of the word *Yada*.

> *But a beautiful cedar palace does not make a great king!*
> *Your father, Josiah, also had plenty to eat and drink.*

But he was just and right in all his dealings. That is why God blessed him. He gave justice and help to the poor and needy, and everything went well for him. Isn't that what it means to know [Yada] me?" says the Lord. (Jeremiah 22:15-16)

In this chapter, Jeremiah (a prophet) is delivering a scathing rebuke to the king of Judah. This king had acted selfishly, neglected the poor and needy, and exploited others to build his kingdom. The Lord tells this corrupt king what it truly means to know (Yada) the Lord. Therein, it was said that to *know* (Yada) meant "doing justice." It also means "showing mercy to the poor and needy" and also means "exemplifying good and righteous *character*".

In other words, *Yada* is the act of faithfully living out our covenant relationship with the Lord in every area of our life, which includes doing justice, showing mercy to the poor and needy, and living an exemplifying good and righteous life—all this down to having the righteousness of God. The life of Joseph is full of all the requirements of spiritual fatherhood (older man), and that explains why he was qualified to be God's dream carrier.

Genesis 37:12-17 showed Joseph to be a boy with a father's heart as he was willing and ready to seek after the well-being of his brothers that hated him. When they were hungry, Joseph showed mercy by accepting to carry out his father's instruction—to take food to his brother—and he lived an exemplifying good and righteous life by feeding his enemy (Proverbs 25:21-22, Romans 12:20). Hence, anyone that can become another Joseph will be qualified by God as God's dream carrier.

Equally, it must be noted that attaining a fatherhood status in the spirit is also about experience. As we know God that is from the beginning and we follow and obey his word and instruction in our daily lives, we grow in experiences, which bring us into full maturity. Each day that passes, we face the wicked one (Satan) in wrestling (Ephesians 6:13), and given that we are men (secondary fatherhood status), we overcome the wicked one. We overcome his imagination, thought, and stronghold. We overcome the temptation of sins and transgressions that he brings to us daily. Oh yes, then we are qualified as older men in the realm of the spirit, and yes, we become God's dream carriers just like Joseph.

In Genesis 37:5-11, Joseph, God's dream carrier, without any effort of his, was given two dreams of the future by God. These dreams were so personal to Joseph, but they were God's dreams in planning stages of how he will bring to pass his promises and covenants that he made with their forefather Abraham.

Both Joseph, his brothers, and even Jacob did not understand that those dreams were not Joseph's selfish ambition; if only they knew that the dreams were God's plans of rescuing them from death in the future, if only they all had a deeper revelation that it was for their overall good, if only they knew that it was a step into the Canaan land that God had promised their father (*watch this!*), they would have celebrated Joseph, they would have pampered him, and they would have kept him in their father's house as a god and not have sold him into slavery, but God's dream through Joseph may not have been actualized.

So also, you, my reader, whenever God gives you dreams, visions, ambitions, business plans, and ideas, and you expect everyone that you share it with to understand you or celebrate you, your God-given visions or dreams may not be actualized. In fact, you must understand that all hatreds, ill-treatments, and oppositions you experienced from those you expected to support your God-given dreams were just indications and vehicles allowed by God to move you on to the actualization of your God-given dream. Be strong and be of good courage, for God knows the plans that he has for you (Jeremiah 29:11).

Do not allow discouraging words or negative words from your oppositions demoralize you. Certainly, Joseph did not allow the negative and irritating attitudes of his brothers to stop him from being in the right frame of mind spiritually, to conceive another God's dream.

When he told them the first dream, he spoke with boldness; their reaction was to hate him. Joseph did not have cold feet and conservation. Joseph did not become all of a sudden fidgety, scarred, sorrowful, and confused. He did not become fearful and gripped by the fear of what man could do to him. He remembered Jeremiah 20:11 that said, "*The Lord is with me like a mighty warrior.*"

Instead, Joseph was very strong because the joy of the Lord became his strength. He was very bold because he remembered Proverbs 28:1 that said that "*the righteous are bold as a lion.*"

Whoa! He was ready for another of God's dreams; in fact, he could not wait to enter a moment of rest (sleep) again to conceive another of God's dreams. I hope I am speaking to another Joseph right now.

Look, I disagreed with the school of thought that blamed Joseph for sharing his dream with his brothers and his parents. Look at it this way: if he had kept the dreams to himself, there may never have been an actualization because with the part ordained to be played by Joseph's brothers in his ordeal, the dreams of God that later got fulfilled in Egypt, may have never come to pass.

If it is true that the steps of the righteous are being ordered by God (Psalm 37:23), I, therefore, believe that Joseph was led by God to share his dreams because dreams are to be shared, even sometimes with difficult and negative people that intend to bring you down, those that swear by their lives that your God-given dreams will never come to pass.

Understand this: if your dream is of God—conceived by your obedience unto God and, in righteousness, inputted by him—be free to share your dreams, your visions with anyone, but be wise and be led by God. It is a fact that many have destroyed their God-given dream by sharing out of arrogance and pride.

Some share their future dreams in the wrong places and to the wrong people because of their inferiority complex; deal with it before it robs you of your God-given dream. Joseph was not recorded to have shared his God-given dream with everyone and everybody that he ran into; he only shared it with those that mattered (though without knowing at the time), those that God had ordained before time immemorial to facilitate and commence the actualization of the dreams.

Please do not make the mistake of opening your mouth everywhere and to everyone just because you want to be accepted and you want to be important before your God's ordained time; such cheap popularity will not last, and the ending may be destructive and disastrous. Joseph could be seen to be filled and led by the Holy Spirit; hence, he knew whom to share his dreams with, and he also knew when to keep his mouth shut. The Bible says in Genesis 37:10 that his father rebukes him, and following the rebuke, Joseph is never heard to throw the weight of his God-given dream around—ever.

One more thing on this area—the Bible recorded that he only shared his dream with his *brothers* and *parents*; in fairness to him, it will be expected that family should be free to share hopes, aspirations, and disappointments, for an ideal family is supposed to be a place where there is love, caring, and fellowship. Is that the case with your fellowships and churches?

One can hold Jacob responsible for the disunity in the family, which he created. Men and women of God, how have you organized the church of God in your care? Is it a safe place for brothers and sisters to share their dreams, hopes, and aspirations, or are your members so afraid of relating to one another because of the disunity, unforgiveness, bitterness, envy, gossip, jealousy, hatred, and even murder that you have knowingly and recklessly allowed to take root in the house of God?

You attend some churches; particularly, if you stay at the back, you will be shocked about the kind of ungodly and unholy discussion that takes place, even when a visiting minister is sweating and preaching his heart out. I was invited to a church special event by the senior pastor of a church recently, and given that I got there some hours late (given my other schedules), I had to seat at the back row. (I was invited to occupy a front seat, but I just felt that God wanted me to stay at the back on that day.) As the prayer was going on powerfully and I was engaged in my prayer, I noticed a church usher and another person chatting away. They were busy gossiping about someone else; may God have mercy.

Oh, in some churches, there is party spirit. Each clique has its groups, and their assignment is to discuss the visiting pastor's shoes, suit, and attire, even while the powerful message is going on. Men and women of God build a church where every member will become a part of God's family; build a church where hopes, visions, dreams, and aspirations are encouraged, lifted up, and assisted. Men and women of God ensure that in all that you teach and, in particular, in all that you do, live a life of example, also ensure that you are there for your brothers and sisters, and let them be able to trust you as their confidants.

The young pastor in your church that is displaying his God-given dreams, spiritual and natural talents and endowments; the brother in the teaching ministry; the deacon and minister that leads prayers, and heaven opens—oh yes, the congregation loves and respects him; they shower him with gifts, and on some occasions, it is like the attention is diverting from you and unto him. Does it really matter?

What matters is that you raised Joseph who conceived God's dreams, and rest assured that if you nurture him, lead him aright, pray for him, and mentor him, whatever God has planned and wherever God makes him, his story will not be complete without your name being mentioned, and one day—maybe, one day—he may be your Joseph that saves Jacob's life and brings him into wealth and prosperity in Egypt.

Therefore, grow mature, act mature, and feel secure. Who knows? The dreams that we fail to celebrate and encourage today may actually be God's dreams for our future when we grow old; your future existence may depend on it. May God help us all.

Final words to all my readers—note the two reactions of the two groups of audiences of Joseph's dreams. With Jacob on one side and Joseph's brothers on the other side, Genesis 37:5 and 11 recorded that while the brothers of Joseph chose to react in hatred and envy, Jacob observed the saying.

The reason for these groups' different reactions can be summed up as follows: Jacob is a father with a fatherly, mature, wise heart while Joseph is a brother, a very young little one with a simple heart. The book of Proverbs referred to them as simple (foolish) that lacked wisdom. In conclusion, rest assured that your group of audience, when sharing your God-given dreams, will always belong to any of the two above.

Some immature brethren—who will become jealous of everyone and anyone that has dreams, visions, brighter future, or achieved better than them—are always envious of anyone that has arrived that God has blessed and that has paid their price in the wilderness; they are the kind of pastors or church members that condemn growing but holiness induced minister or church while Jacob's group is the mature-in-depth Christians that walk in God's kind of wisdom.

They have been taught and they have learnt that promotion does not come from the west, east, nor south, but from God. They understand the principle of godliness that says, "Submit yourself under the mighty hand of God and he will exalt you at his appointed time." Oh yes, they are Jacob; they will be observant, and they will be quick to hear but slow to judge, slow to give criticisms. As a result, their input in your life will be sound and invaluable.

Unfortunately, the brethren's group could be members and could be ministers of God that you even call spiritual parents while Jacob could be members and or your spiritual leaders. You, therefore, need God's discerning Spirit to know who is who, and when you can differentiate, rely more on Jacob's group and be careful with the brothers' group.

CHAPTER 5

The Plot of Evil

But they saw him in the distance, and before he reached them, they plotted to kill him. "Here comes that dreamer!" they said to each other. "Come now, let's kill him and throw him into one of these cisterns and say that a ferocious animal devoured him. Then we'll see what comes of his dreams." When Reuben heard this, he tried to rescue him from their hands. "Let's not take his life," he said. "Don't shed any blood. Throw him into this cistern here in the wilderness, but don't lay a hand on him." Reuben said this to rescue him from them and take him back to his father.

—Genesis 37:18-22

We must all understand that the plot of evil has become part of our world since the day that the first Adam fell in the Garden of Eden. The Bible recorded that after they were driven out of this garden, they gave birth to sons that came before God to sacrifice. Due to hatred and jealousy, Cain plotted within him to kill his brother, Abel, and he actually did kill him. Since then, brothers have been plotting against brothers, sisters against sisters, even in the body of Christ; may the Lord deliver us.

So it was not a surprise when the demon of jealousy and hatred resurfaced again in the case of Joseph and his brothers. Born of the same father, they shared the same DNA, but while Joseph was a carrier of God's dream, the others were carriers of the demon of jealousy and hatred. The Bible said in Genesis 37:18 that when they saw him from afar off, they conspired against him to kill him; they wanted to kill him, thinking that once he was killed, his dream would not come to pass. There is some spiritual revelation that God wants us to take from this situation.

We must understand that though the brothers of Joseph were the culprits of this conspiracy, there was a demon operating inside of them to ensure that God's dream will not come to pass; they were just unfree agents forced into obedience by the principal demons that engaged their mind. They were slaves to the spirit that enslaved their minds—spirit of jealousy, rivalry, conspiracy, and hatred (Matthew 6:24, Romans 6:16, Ephesians 2:2).

Are you also enslaved by the spirit of jealousy, rivalry, conspiracy, and hatred? Do you hate your brothers and sisters? The Bible says in the book of 1 John 4:20 that anyone that hates his brother does not love God and the book of Leviticus 19:17 commands us not to hate our brother. I, therefore, implore you today that you should yield to the command of God for the sake of the dream of his that is inside of you.

And to those who, right now, are going through what Joseph went through in the hands of his brothers and to those that have been victims of relative abuses, my word of encouragement to you is that you yield your pains to the Lord Jesus Christ in prayer; only he can cure all our infirmities. Seek godly counselling, and forgive your abusers quickly through the enabling power of the Holy Spirit so that you will not be trapped forever in the prison of self-pity, guilt, and victim mode, and let go and let God, for you are pregnant with God's dream; you have no other space for bitterness, malice, and rancour.

CHAPTER 6

God's Dreamer and the Enemies' Pit

And it came to pass, when Joseph was come unto his brethren, that they stript Joseph out of his coat, his coat of many colours that was on him; And they took him, and cast him into a pit: and the pit was empty, there was no water in it. And they sat down to eat bread: and they lifted up their eyes and looked, and, behold, a company of Ishmaelite came from Gilead with their camels bearing spicery and balm and myrrh, going to carry it down to Egypt. And Judah said unto his brethren, what profit is it if we slay our brother, and conceal his blood? Come, and let us sell him to the Ishmaelite, and let not our hand be upon him; for he is our brother and our flesh. And his brethren were content.

—Genesis 37:23-27

Readers will note the sequence of events that took place in the passage above. The Bible said that the brothers of Joseph stripped Joseph out of his coat of many colours. It must be understood that though the brothers of Joseph were physically responsible for carrying out this act on Joseph, there was a spirit responsible for it—this was called the spirit of the air. Ephesians 2:2.

The Bible says this spirit works in the hearts of the disobedient, and its aims are to steal the dream of the righteous, kill them if they can, and destroy their minds John 10:10. So also, children of God, this is a warning to us all; ensure that you do not allow the enemy to steal your God-given dream, no matter what they throw at you. The spiritual meaning of the robe of many colours that Joseph's brothers took from Joseph is called righteousness. Isaiah 61:10, Job 29:14.

We, as Christians, must ensure that we do not allow the enemies of our soul to disrobe us of the coat of righteousness that God has given to us. The Bible made us know, in the case of Abraham, that he (Abraham) believed God, and it was counted unto him as righteousness. Romans 4:3. But how can you and I ensure that our God-given robe of righteousness is not robbed by the enemies of our soul?

It must be noted that though they were successful in removing Joseph's natural garment, they were ignorant of the fact that Joseph's real garment was within; they were also ignorant of the fact that the outer garment was just a symbol of his growing inner fruit of righteousness that qualified him to receive an outer coat from his father.

The outer coats in the life of a believer are the additions that God promised to give us when we have sought after righteousness (Matthew 6:33). These include all material benefits of life, such as cars, clothing, money, wealth, children, health, and in the worse scenario, just like he was permitted to strip Joseph of his coat of many colours.

We must ensure that, as God's dreamers, we do not allow the enemies of our soul strip us of what really matters—our coat of righteousness—irrespective of any natural blessing we may take on our journey unto the fulfilment of God's dream in us.

I can feel Joseph saying, "Brothers, you are making a mistake—what makes me God's dreamer is within and not without. This coat of many colours that you are taking right now is just the indication of who I am within." Can you and I, as believers that have received the righteousness of God, speak like Joseph in the days of trial, when we attend interviews where the boss is promising to give us the employment letter only if we have a one-night stand with him or her? Can we speak as Joseph when we are threatened with a sack letter unless we compromise and violate our conscience and God? When the enemies of our soul are after our outer coat (jobs, health, wealth, etc.), can we still hold on to our righteousness in God even when our outer coat is taken?

Can you and I still continue to obey God even when it seems that God has completely failed us? Can we still continue to hope in him, believe in his spoken and written word? Can we still continue to pray to him even when our last prayer seems to have not been answered? I encourage you, my reader, to be another Joseph, a man that has put on the coat of righteousness; hence, when life and family disrobed him of his outer, protective clothing, he was not naked. Oh no, he was not vulnerable;

in fact, he was fully covered. Joseph was wearing the robe of righteousness, which only God gives only to those that always believe him and demonstrates their faith by their obedience to his word.

The Bible recorded in verse 24 that they cast him into a pit. The question is why a blood brother would cast his younger brother who came to attend to their welfare into a pit. The answer is in verse 22 above; God was at work in Reuben to save Joseph's life from early death. Note this: Reuben was part of the rebellion from the start, and he also hated Joseph because of his dream, but God created a state of division between the brothers in order to save Joseph's life God took over the eldest of the brothers and, by so doing, weakened the strong emotion of anger that demanded for the life of Joseph. Throughout the plan to terminate the life of Joseph, God was in control, for the Bible says that the counsel of God shall stand (Psalm 33:11, Isaiah 46:10, and Proverbs 19:21).

The counsel of God is that Joseph will rule over them, that they will serve him, bow to him, and take orders from him; how will this come to pass if their plot to kill Joseph becomes successful? In a like manner, concerning your life, you must know that the counsel of God shall stand, irrespective of any evil plot masterminded by the devil's agents (humans or demons) or even Satan himself. If it will not work for your good and work towards achieving the original plan of God for your life, the Lord will thwart the plans. Just as he used Reuben to confuse and disorganise an evil plot of murdering Joseph, the Lord will use the enemies themselves to work against their own plots and rescue you.

I strongly believe that Joseph, a righteous man, had a deep understanding of God, his ways, and his power and ability to influence all things, both in heaven and on earth. That, I submit, is the rationale behind Joseph's peaceful solace even in the face of adversity. All throughout the ordeal of a plot to murder Joseph, he was not moved, and he was not worried, either. When they decided to throw him into a pit, Joseph was calm and unshaken, even in the midst of dreadful enemies, because he knew that he was the carrier of God's dream; hence, God had every reason and responsibility to protect him.

For so many of us that God has loaded with heavenly dreams, God's dreams, it is sad to note that at every attack of the enemy, even at shouting of the roaring lion that seeks whom to devour, we become roughened, worried, and in some cases, fearful. No, we should be strong, bold, and calm like Joseph.

We must have this understanding in us that if the dream inside of us is of God, it is like a woman who is married to a powerful king; when the woman is pregnant and the pregnancy belongs to the king, you can be sure that the king will do everything within his power to ensure that his wife and his unborn babe are always safe.

So also is the God of heaven—the almighty God; omnipotent, omniscient and omnipresent God; the might in battle, the King of kings and the Lord of lords; the everlasting father; the ancient of days; the lion of the tribe of Judah; and the unchanging changer. He will ensure that his dream inside of you is intact and safe, and he will also see to it that you, God's dream carrier, are equally at safety. Hence, you must always call into remembrance, just as King Hezekiah, that the battle (your battle as God's dream carrier) is of the Lord, and God has never lost a battle—no, not in the past, not now, and not forever. So be still and know that he is the Lord.

Another lesson for every God's dream carrier can be found in verse 24. The Bible recorded that they took Joseph's robe of many colours, and Joseph let them without any struggle or fight. Dream carriers that fight with life always end up as victim; let God fight for you. Are you going through persecution and affliction in your husband's house? Do you have an in-law problem, or are your stepparents making life so difficult for you? Let go and let God; commit it all unto God.

In this kind of situation, one will expect Joseph to swear at them, curse them, bite them, and kick them; this may have made matters worse for Joseph. Rather, he let them have the day; it was painful, yes, but he endured the pain. He allowed God, the perfect avenger, to avenge him; let God avenge you. But God will only avenge those that do it according to his word, those that will not justify their reaction based on the action of others.

The Bible taught us to pray for those that despitefully use us, and even pray for our enemies because, by so doing, we heap a hot fire on them. I employ everyone that carries God's dreams to ensure that you do not allow any root of bitterness inside of you—this, if allowed to grow, will cause your God's planted dream to be miscarried. So love your enemy, and ask God for his grace to love them and to pray for those that despitefully use you, for as the Lord lives, I decree into your current situation, as an Abraham of this generation and a prophet of the living God, you shall have the last laugh. (Your *amen* is too small; say a bigger *amen*.)

Note again in verse 24, the Bible recorded that they cast him (Joseph) into an empty pit. I want you to picture in your mind a young lad, who has been through a great ordeal of a death threat, under a very hot sun in a desert, now being cast into a pit without water. You can imagine how hot the pit will be, certainly very hot, and God allowed his dream carrier to be cast into a dangerous pit without doing anything to provide immediate rescue? Yes, for the way of God is not the same as man.

There may be time and time again when you, as God's dream carrier, will be allowed to be cast into a pit by the enemy; the pit of Joseph was a form of a dungeon, with the aim to restrict his journey into the actualisation of his God-given dream. In today's interpretation, the pit may be a form of setback thrown our way by the devil, his demons, and humans that allowed him to use them. The aims of this pit are to restrict our movement, stop us in our tracks, create a diversion, cause confusion, and kill the dreams within. Notwithstanding the challenges, remember that if God refuses to intervene, he certainly has a better plan, and it will work for your good as a call of God and because you love him.

Joseph did not struggle with his brothers when they were casting him into the pit; he was not disturbed while in the pit, and neither did he beg his brothers for him to be removed from the pit. Instead, he put his trust in the Lord, his God. He knew that struggling would cause him more damage and calling his natural father would be fruitless because his father was not nearby. He has been taught that the arm of the flesh will always fail. But one thing I am sure he must have done at every stage of this difficulty and ordeal of his life is that, certainly, he must have called on God of his Abraham, God of Isaac, and God of his father, Jacob.

I encourage every reader of this treasure book to please ensure that whenever you are faced with oppositions, challenges, and difficulties in the journey that has been set before you, whenever the devil casts you into a pit, should the devil, humans, or demons attempt to restrict your God-given vision through affliction of sickness, unemployment, divorce, separation, homelessness, and the likes, just like Joseph, know that this is the time to talk to God regularly in prayer and listen to him speak to you in his word. Pray and ensure that you pray through, and that God that rescued Joseph from an impossible situation will rescue you too.

In verse 25, it could be stated that God's next move in disguise set in. Listen to me. God is still in control, no matter how bad or bleak it may look or seem. The Bible recorded that the band of Ishmaelites was coming along. The devil, through Joseph's brothers, had attempted to stalemate the progressive plan of God by casting Joseph into a dry pit, so Joseph's journey, although he was alive and well, had come to a dead end as far as the enemy was concerned. He could only go around in circles within the perimeter of the pit.

The devil's plot was to allow Joseph to move around in the pit, so Joseph felt and seemed to be progressive in the pit; Joseph could move forward and back in the pit but only at a lower underground level where no one could see him. It was like a covering cast placed on Joseph, his progress, and his God-given dream. But God—in his wisdom, power, and might—set out the journey of the Ishmaelites towards the scene of the pit and inserted into the hearts of those wicked brothers of Joseph the thought of making profit. It may seem equally sad to see brothers cashing in on selling their brother into slavery, but in the eyes of God, this is a journey to the right ordained places.

So also, we must know that in every situation that you and I call a bad dead end, the Bible says in the book of 1 Corinthians 10:13 that God will always make a way of escape so that we can be able to bear it; so continue to trust God, just like Joseph did, and your way of escape will come shortly in Jesus' name.

Has life sold you, my reader, into a journey of slavery or mingled you with a class of total strangers called Ishmaelites? Or have you been betrayed by those that you relied on, trusted, or tried to help? Remember, God is still in control, and he has a plan. I have heard stories of relatives that were helped and accommodated, and such relatives later defrauded their benefactor by abusing their bank cards. I have also heard of close friends that snatched their friend's husbands and wives and many shocking stories. Unto such, I have a word of prophesy for you—you shall laugh again. Realise that God knows about your troubles, and he will not allow you to go through more than what you can bear, for he will make a way of escape for you.

While still on this chapter, the Lord brought the following divine revelation to me: Just as Joseph was cast into the pit by his family members to dehydrate and then die, so also is the case with many of God's dream carriers who have failed to deaden or mortify their members (sinful natures, "family within the natural Adamic body"), which are, on the earth, fornication, uncleanness, inordinate affection, evil concupiscence, and covetousness, which is idolatry. Colossians 3:5.

It is, therefore, a necessary obligation as ordered by God that you, as God's dream carrier, must ensure that you deaden, kill, and mortify your members (fleshly members—not your body parts, but your fleshly Adamic members that were infused into your body through the disobedience of our first natural father in the Garden of Eden), which, according to the book of Colossians 3:5, include fornication, uncleanness, inordinate affection, evil concupiscence, and covetousness. You must realize that your failure to destroy these demonically infused members, introduced by the devil, may lead to severe, catastrophic consequences.

Just as the brothers of Joseph cast him into the pit to die, these family members too have aims and objectives set by their master, the devil, and that is to cast their host into pits of no fulfillment of God's dream, into the pit of discouragement, into the pit of no progress, spiritual miscarriage, spiritual abortion, and spiritual and physical death. John 10:10.

These spiritual family members are assigned by the devil to cause spiritual death, which is separation from God's word, his Spirit, his direction, and his revelation; the consequence of this is that such individual will be left dry with no regular supply from God and eventually withered off as urgent assistance is not provided. This way, many vision and dream carriers have lost their God-given dreams and visions; they are now left with memories of God's promises that have not materialized all because they chose to keep the wrong parasite, which God required to be destroyed. Why? Because they are enemies in disguise, agents of the devil.

Picture in your mind a child in the womb that has not received the required supplies from her mother because the mother has not received all required supplies due to famine; you will agree with me that if urgent attention and steps are not taken to rectify the situation, both the mother and her child will be a waste. Likewise, any of God's dreamer that continues to permit the forbidden members, which God instructed to be terminated, to live in them runs the risk of the above spiritual catastrophe. Please, God's dream carriers, ensure that you are not casualties of the devil and his infused spiritually sinful members.

CHAPTER 7

God's Dreamer and the Unknown Journey

So when the Midianite merchants came by, his brothers pulled Joseph up out of the cistern and sold him for twenty shekels of silver to the Ishmaelites, who took him to Egypt. When Reuben returned to the cistern and saw that Joseph was not there, he tore his clothes. He went back to his brothers and said, "The boy isn't there! Where can I turn now?" Then they got Joseph's robe, slaughtered a goat and dipped the robe in the blood. They took the ornate robe back to their father and said, "We found this. Examine it to see whether it is your son's robe." He recognized it and said, "It is my son's robe! Some ferocious animal has devoured him. Joseph has surely been torn to pieces." Then Jacob tore his clothes, put on sackcloth and mourned for his son many days. All his sons and daughters came to comfort him, but he refused to be comforted. "No," he said, "I will continue to mourn until I join my son in the grave." So his father

wept for him. Meanwhile, the Midianite sold Joseph in
Egypt to Potiphar, one of Pharaoh's officials, the captain
of the guard.

—Genesis 37:28-36

While I was prayerfully preparing to write this chapter, I originally selected a different heading that, humanly speaking, I thought would sum up this chapter, but at a point, it was very clear in me that the Holy Spirit had another heading for this chapter. As I began to seek his face, the above heading now in place came to my understanding, and the more I read it, the more I have a conviction in my spirit that this is where some readers of this book are right now. I mean, the title of the chapter may actually be speaking of you.

Oh yes! You are currently on an unknown journey right now, and to make it worse, you are surrounded by strangers who may not understand your challenges and what you are going through within, but I got very good news for you: God that made you, that knows your substance even when you were hidden in your mother's womb, knows where you are, and he understands what you are going through.

Oh! He saw Jonah in the belly of the fish; even the dark night could not hide the whereabouts of Jacob when God decided to change his name and release the blessing of Abraham unto him. The God that knew the locations where life and people had hidden David, and when it was time to bring him to the throne, he fetched him out; that God that made a conference in the fire with the three Hebrews when Nebuchadnezzar banished them to death via his fire; that God that attended to the lions even before Daniel was thrown therein—he knows where you are.

The God that knew the location of the fountain source of the Red Sea and was able to reach it in good time, in spite of the volume of dark water that enveloped it, and instantly made an express road in the Red Sea to enable his people (Israel) a way of escape will make a way of escape for you.

This God that made the Jordan River flee, he is the God that can see clearly even in the darkest hour. He knows the part that you tread; he knows where life, people, and challenges have taken you; he understands even what nobody can, and he sends me to you as his prophet. *"For I know the plans that I have concerning you, to give you a future and something to hope for"* *Jeremiah 29:11.*

The Bible recorded in Genesis 37:28 that Joseph was pulled up. One can imagine the sign of relief on the face of Joseph when he discovered unexpectedly that there was an elevation; he thought, *Whoa! Freedom at last.* But he never knew that this was not freedom as he deserved but rather a betrayal and the beginning into an unknown long journey with total strangers.

Are you, today, in Joseph's shoes? Do you feel like you are just moving from one problem into another? As you thought that it was all over, all of a sudden, another challenge had taken you over. You were not alone; even Joseph felt that way during his ordeal, but at the back of your mind, just like Joseph, remember that God is with you if, indeed, you are carrying his dream, and his favour will go with you every step of the way. You must also call to mind that God has a plan and only his counsel shall stand; it shall surely work for your good.

Before they lifted him up from the pit, they referred to him as their brother and their flesh, but the devil had blinded their conscience so much; hence, they never thought of the pains and heartaches they later caused to both Joseph and their parents, who was later deceived that Joseph was dead. It seemed an evil thing for them to take the life of a brother and their flesh, but it seemed right to sell him off into a bleak future for monetary gain.

Are you the kind of person that will sell your family member to make money? Are you the selfish type that just wants anything and everything at all cost, irrespective of what prices others must pay for you to get it? You are a prototype of Joseph's brothers; change today before it is too late.

The Bible recorded that Joseph's brothers lifted him up but sold him into slavery. They lifted him up from the pit of limitation but with another plan and agenda to sell him into slavery. As you read this treasure book, God is bringing forth a revelation here, which is the following: it is not every lifting up that is truly God sent. Every help from the arms of flesh will always come with a tag, a price too expensive to pay. There is always a hidden agenda; whenever the devil opens some doors for man, it always comes at a much cost. The cost to Adam and Eve was the discovery of their nakedness, homelessness, and curses. We must, therefore, be vigilant and ensure that we do not get carried away and begin to dance to the tune of man and flesh; it is always a very costly price to pay. Remember, there is always a hidden agenda.

So they sold him. They disconnected him from the family he was born into, and they rendered him fatherless violently, without any consideration of the fact that he no longer had a mother. They were selfish and cruel; they only thought of financial gain to themselves; what about the pain of being forced into a future that Joseph did not choose in the first place?

They made his decision for him without consulting him. They barged into his life without permission and made personal decisions regarding relocation for him; to make it worse; he was not even permitted to make a contribution into the matter that strictly concerned him and his future life. Oh, they did not only sell Joseph into a forced journey for money but also failed to consider the feelings of their father, who, indeed, loved his son.

I believe that the Holy Spirit, deep down inside of me, is convinced that this is for someone reading this treasure book. Oh yes, sometimes in your past, you had been abused by relatives who were meant to protect you. In another case, someone or people in your past, without your consent, had made unfavorable decisions based on selfish reasons, and this meant your detriment. There is someone right now reading through this book—you were forced into an arranged marriage without your consent, opinion, and approval.

You are also reading this book, and I perceive that your marriage has been one-sided. You have been dominated by your spouse, who vowed before man and God to love you on your wedding day; rather than love, you experience intimidation. You are forced and put under duress to comply with your spouse's selfish desire, and you are constantly put under the fear of divorce if you fail to comply with what they want. This has put you under stress and constant agitation and fear, and you now feel like a prisoner in the love you thought will surround you with freedom.

I have got good news for you: Joseph also experienced similar situations from his family and relatives, but he handled it in God's way. The Bible says in the book of Proverbs 3:5-6 that you should "Trust in the Lord with all thine heart; and lean not unto thine own understanding and in all your ways acknowledge him, and he shall direct your paths." This was the mind-set of Joseph when he was going through his challenges.

First, Joseph *trusted the Lord with all his heart,* and hence, there was calmness in his spirit man. Secondly, he did *not lean upon his own understanding* as he allowed God to figure out the way of escape for him. Thirdly, in all his ways and within his spirit man, in prayer and by faith, Joseph *acknowledged God*; consequently, God *directed his paths* unto becoming the prime minister of Egypt with the only important vote of the king, unopposed.

The following are just some few words on the steps that Joseph took when he was going though his challenges and the result that only God can bring out of a terrible and challenging situation:

God's Dreamer—Your Three Parts to Perform

1. Trust the Lord with Your Heart

To trust in God as Joseph did, it must be understood that there must have been a deep relationship of love for a real trust to develop. Therefore, it is very important and necessary for you as God's dream carrier to have developed a deep relationship with God through his son. This is to say that you have been saved through the blood of Jesus. This means that in a particular day, a time, and in a place, you heard the word of God, and you repented of your sins, and you invited Jesus into your life as your personal Lord and Saviour.

If you have done this at a point in the past, I wish to congratulate and encourage you for the best and most important decision of life, and I shall introduce you to the other part of trusting in the Lord shortly; however, if you have not come through the cross, I mean, if you have not accepted the Lord Jesus Christ into your life as your Saviour, this may be your long-awaited opportunity to do so; please take this chance now, and be born into the family of God.

I heard you say, "Yes, Prophet, I want to give my life to Jesus." Say these words after me:

Lord Jesus, I know that I am a sinner and in need of your forgiveness. I agree that I have sinned against you, but I ask you to, please, forgive me and take away all my sins. Please come into my heart, and take away the pains in my life.

I want to know and have you as my Lord, Saviour, and my God; please start a relationship with me today.

Come into my heart, and show me your presence in a very real way. I believe in my heart and I confess with my mouth that you are my Saviour and my Lord. I thank you, my Lord that you have chosen me today to be your son. Please come and fill me with your Holy Spirit. I vow to serve you today and forever with all my heart. In Jesus' name, I pray. (Amen.)

If you have sincerely and truthfully said these words of prayer above from your heart, I congratulate you today, and I welcome you into the family of God. Today, you are born again, and your name is written in the book of life. Do you know that there is joy in heaven right now because you have chosen to become a child of God?

The other side of trusting in the Lord is to ensure that you have Jesus Christ also as your Lord, but how? I heard you say, "By being led by the Holy Spirit on a daily basis." For the Bible said that many that are being led by the Holy Spirit are sons of God. The more you are led by the Holy Spirit and seeing that he always leads you right, you will realize that your trust in him will grow the more. Trust grows over the years of a loving relationship.

2. Do Not Lean Upon Your Own Understanding

This is an instruction from God to everyone that carries his dream. The instruction is that you must not lean upon your own understanding. Why? Because man understanding is very porous and fragmented because the understanding of man is limited and unreliable without God, and lastly, because every man or woman's understanding is without knowledge of God as the devil is the brain behind it. A very good example is the case of Eve relying on her understanding in respect to eating the forbidden fruit in the garden. At the point when

Eve was not relying on God, she was, in fact, relying on information provided by the serpent (inspired by Satan), and the consequences of such reliance were God's curses and both natural and spiritual death.

3. Acknowledge God

Another necessary requirement for every God's dream carrier is to ensure that they acknowledge God. To acknowledge God means to put him as number one in everything, just like David, who will not take any steps in life without seeking God's face. Consequentially, he was led by God, and his steps were ordered by him.

God's Usual Response—God Will Direct Your Path

Whenever God's dream carrier demonstrates his or her trust in God and refuses to lean upon his or her own porous and sensual understanding but, instead, chooses to acknowledge God, the result that normally follows is that such person will always see God direct their path. We all need God's direction, and so do you; hence, you must see to it that you do your part so that God can do his own part.

Truly, the step of Joseph was ordered even though it may not seem like that from the onset. Joseph escaped death and ended in a pit. While he was stuck in the pit with little or no progress, all of a sudden, he was lifted up from the pit, only to be sold into the hands of strangers who, again, sold him into permanent slavery; but the point was that this was how God ordered it to be, and it could not be done in any other way.

So also, you must know that irrespective of anything and all things that you go through as God's dream carrier, understand that it is part of the processes that God has set up in his plan, if only you love God (loving God means doing your parts as stated above—"If you love me, you shall keep my commandment," says Jesus) and are called according to his purpose. For real, it will work for your good at the end of it all.

Lastly, on this chapter, one can see God's orchestrated protocol arrangement of Joseph into the house of Potiphar. Joseph could have been sold unto any other family but Potiphar, and who knows, Joseph's setup may not have yielded God's desired plans. But because God was in charge of Joseph's life's protocol services, Joseph could not fall into the wrong hands. So also with you, if you ensure that you allow God to be God in respective of the situation, you will discover, with time, that God has a plan that is totally for your good.

CHAPTER 8

God's Dreamer in Slavery

*Then there passed by Midianites merchantmen; and
they drew and lifted up Joseph out of the pit, and sold
Joseph to the Ishmaelites for twenty pieces of silver: and
they brought Joseph into Egypt.*

—Genesis 37:28

*And Joseph was brought down to Egypt; and Potiphar,
an officer of Pharaoh, captain of the guard, an
Egyptian, bought him of the hands of the Ishmaelites,
which had brought him down thither. And the LORD
was with Joseph, and he was a prosperous man; and
he was in the house of his master the Egyptian. And his
master saw that the LORD was with him, and that the
LORD made all that he did to prosper in his hand. And
Joseph found grace in his sight, and he served him: and
he made him overseer over his house, and all that he
had he put into his hand. And it came to pass from the
time that he had made him overseer in his house, and*

over all that he had, that the LORD blessed the Egyptian's
house for Joseph's sake; and the blessing of the LORD was
upon all that he had in the house, and in the field. And
he left all that he had in Joseph's hand; and he knew
not ought he had, save the bread which he did eat. And
Joseph was a goodly person, and well favoured.

—Genesis 39:1-6

It must be noted that as Joseph was breathing a sigh of relief
that "Yes! It is all over," all of a sudden, "Oh!—there was a
change of plan." Although no more death, he would never see
his family members again; it was time for a long journey with
total strangers. Yes, Joseph did not fight either his brothers or
the Ishmaelite strangers; rather, he trusted in his God and held
on to his dream. He was fully assured of the fact that he was
God's dream carrier and that God's sole duty was to set out the
modalities of how the dream would come to fulfilment.

Joseph saw the arrival of the Ishmaelites and the sale of himself
to them as God's plan to rescue him from sudden death. How
do you read into the challenges that come your way, dream
carriers? How do you interpret the twists and turns of life that
God allows to interrupt the enemy's plans? Do you even see
God at work, or do you always blame him for failing to act?

Joseph understands that for him to give birth to the dream of
God inside of him, there are some processes to undergo. He
knows fully that for there to be a desired result, he must be willing
to persevere, tolerate, endure many things, and allow patience
to have her full work in him so that he will lack nothing (James

1:4). So also, my godly counsel to you today is that you should let Patience have her perfect work in you, that you may be perfect and entire, wanting nothing. The grace to take this advice—may the good Lord shower it on you in Jesus' name. (Amen.)

Do note that it is very normal for a person carrying God's dream to be sold by life into more challenges of life; oh, from the hands of the Ishmaelites into the house of Potiphar in Egypt, Joseph started a new life in slavery. Generally speaking, once in this situation, sometimes, it may be humanly possible to think that there is no way out.

Oh yes, when Joseph found himself in Egypt, he thought, *you know what? This is it, this is where I will die,* particularly, when he built rapport with other slaves and they advised him of how long they have been in slavery. Some were brought from Europe; some were brought from Africa, while some were brought from Asia to be sold into slavery in the first civilized part of the world, Egypt. The conclusion was "Never again I shall taste freedom."

Is that speaking of you right now in the mess you find yourself, in the challenges of unemployment, huge debt, and broken home and broken marriages? Is the enemy showing you every other victim of his that has been in his trap for donkey's years, and is he telling you that this sickness has no cure and, therefore, you shall die? I got a message for you: the devil is a liar and the father of all lies, so cut his bluff.

Remember that he may afflict others but not you. Why? Because you are an eagle, not a chicken; you are destined by God to fly and soar through this storm, even through the eye of the storm.

You are made to look unto the sun straight in the eye, and damn the consequences. You shall come out of this. God himself, who will not give you more than what you can bear, has promised to make a way of escape. So relax; God is in control, even in the school where the devil seems to be the tutor.

Verse 1 of the thirty-ninth chapter of the book of Genesis started with Joseph being brought down to Egypt. Though Egypt, as of then, was the most civilized country of the world, it was recorded that the journey of Joseph, just like Abraham and Isaac's journeys, was a process of going down. (The difference between Abraham, Isaac, and Joseph's journey was that while the former came down to Egypt by choice, the latter came into Egypt by force.)

So also, you, as God's dream carrier, may find yourself going down, but with God on your side, the depth of your sliding down is only an indication of how high God will take you. Remember, whenever a skyrocketing building is to be constructed, the foundation must be very deep.

God set up Potiphar to buy Joseph from the Ishmaelites. Are you being bought over today? As you thought you had come to the end of one situation, another one took over. My advise to you today is humble yourself under the mighty hand of God so that at his appointed time, he will exalt you.

In spite of the changeovers and transitions that were occurring in the life of Joseph, he refused to lose sight of the most important thing. Verse 2 of chapter 39 says, "And God was with Joseph," and I strongly believe that for a teenager of seventeen years to be able to endure this ordeal, it is very clear that he has a deep conviction that God is with him.

And God was with Joseph? So why did this God allow him to go through all this ordeal, why did God allow his brothers to sell him off into slavery, why didn't God stop them, why didn't God stop either the Ishmaelites or Potiphar in Egypt, and why was God passive instead of active throughout the difficult journey of Joseph? These and many more are the questions that I have heard many ask today, in particular, when you tell them that God loves them.

They say things like "Where was God when I lost my job?" "Where was God when my home was broken and my marriage ended up in a divorce?" "Why didn't God stop my dad, mum, sister, brother, or loved one from dying?" and "Why didn't God answer my prayer when I prayed and asked for help?" These are deep questions from a heart that is bleeding with the pain of helplessness, and may be, this is where you are today. I have an answer for you: God was there all along, working it out for your good. The fact that you do not see him visibly or that you do not hear him does not mean that God is not there or that he has not done what he is supposed to have done.

Job says, *"Behold, I go forward, but he is not there; and backward, but I cannot perceive him: on the left hand, where he doth work, but I cannot behold him: he hideth himself on the right hand, that I cannot see him" (Job 23:8-9).* Permit me to say at this junction that there are many times we cause the predicament that we find ourselves in; some of the situations and challenges that we face arise as results of our willful or reckless disobedience to God's perfect will.

So many Christians are working in the permissive will of God, and when the repercussion arrives, we then expect God to attend to us and sort the mess out. No, sir or ma'am, it does not work like that. The father of the prodigal son had all the material resources, logistics, and networks to search for his missing and lost prodigal son, but he never did. Why? Because the prodigal son left home in the permissive will of the father. Yes, the father loved him so much, and he longed for the day he shall return, but the best the father could do was to wait at home, looking through the window, for the day when his son shall come back to his senses and return to his root. So also does God; whenever you do anything in his permissive will, you will pay the price of your desire and your decision, for the serpent will bite whoever breaks the edge.

To those that are asking or seeking to know what it means to be operative in God's permissive will and what the perfect will of God is, the answer is very simple, and it is in Proverbs 3:5. Any Christian that trusts in God and his word and looks up to his Spirit to order his or her daily steps is walking in God's perfect will, but anyone that relies on their own understanding is walking in God's permissive will. Such will make decisions on their own accord, and they want God to rubber-stamp it.

This matter cannot be fully laid to rest until I make this point: There may be time and time again when God's dream carrier, who walks in God's perfect will just like Joseph, will find themselves in difficult times that heaven seems to be silent;

in such occasions, I encourage you to trust in your God, your Lord, who says in the book of Jeremiah 29:11, *"For I know the plans that I have concerning you, the plans of good and not of evil, to give you a future and something to hope for."* If it does not seem like it today, please continue to wait for it. God is not a man that he should lie or a son of man that he should go back on his word. The vision actualization is for an appointed time; though it tarries, please wait for it. The process does not really matter once the desired result has occurred.

The Bible said in verse 2 that the Lord was with Joseph even in the slavery nest that life had brought him down on; down in Egypt, God was with him. This shows that it does not really count where life, situations, challenges, people, and difficulties have placed you, and neither does any label that you have been labeled with matter. What really counts is that the Lord is with you; hence, you are not alone, and you are so sure that you will come out at his appointed time.

That explains why David, in the book of Psalms 23, says, though he walks in the valley of the shadow of death, he shall fear no evil, for God is with him. Just like Joseph in slavery, who has lost all human dignity and identity and is now in Egypt, he is only known as "slave boy." Notwithstanding, the God of heaven and earth identified with his lowest state; what a God!

When you are God's dream carrier, even though you will go through God's ordained processes (so that godly characters and fruits can be grown inside of you), notwithstanding whatever you have to go through in your journey, he will surely be with you, and if God is with you, there are some undeniable blessings that must occur in your life.

Firstly, you shall be prosperous, just like Joseph whom God made to prosper in Genesis 39:2. Tell me why Joseph would not be prosperous when God, whose middle name is *prosperity*, was with him. Irrespective of how based life has relocated you or maybe you have lost your job, your marriage, your family member, etc., God will always be with you. Has life reduced you to a menial-job man even with your highly qualified certificates? Listen to me: what matters is that wherever and whatever you find yourself doing, ensure that God is there and in it with you for real, and in his time, you must prosper.

Secondly, everyone will see that the Lord is by your side. In verse 3 of the above chapter, the Bible said that Joseph's master saw that God was with him. Do you know, believers, that if, indeed, you are right with God, even in the lowest ebb that you find yourself, some people who are better placed than you in your place of work will envy you because they will see God with you; they will see the beauty of God, and the satisfaction and contentment that surround your existence will marvel them. Why? Because it is unnatural but supernatural, denoting God's presence that gives *rest*.

I remember when I was working as a housing officer for a local authority in London many years ago: Even though I was on modest salary, my senior managers were envious of me, and they always would say it to my face that I was a wealthy man and that the modest salary I was on then was not my main income. Why? All because they saw the achievement that my heavenly

Father had brought into my life, even with my modest salary. May this good God stick with you in times of your challenges and give you his *rest* in Jesus' name (say a bigger *amen*).

Thirdly, again, in verse 3, the Bible said that Joseph's master equally saw that his God also made all he did to prosper. It is not only that the gentiles in your office, your unbelieving neighbours near your home will see God through you, but they will also discover, recognize, and understand that your God has made you prosper.

I submit to you at this stage that Joseph must have been living a godly life in the house of his master for Potiphar to have seen his God. Joseph must have been a living testimony; oh, I can see Joseph on a daily basis, sharing his faith in the God of Abraham with everyone (including Potiphar) that cares to listen. Joseph was not afraid of his master, and neither was he beaten by the change of culture and environment.

Oh yes, Joseph lived for God; no wonder he was not alone in a strange land. He saw God every day, he talked with God, and he listened and heard God's voice every minute and every second; wherever Joseph went, God went with him, and they were two bonded friends. The master saw Joseph, and everywhere he saw Joseph, he also saw God. When Joseph was given a household task to do, God too got involved; if the task was too hard for a young boy like Joseph to accomplish, God stepped in and got his hands dirty. All this was at the full view of Potiphar. Equally noticeable too was the outcome of Joseph's effort in the house of Potiphar; it can be summed up in few words—*prosperous man*, for God was with him.

So also, my reader, if you are willing, right now, to live for Christ in your place of work, oh, if you are ready to allow your life to minister Christ, if you will share the testimony of the risen Christ through your godly fruit, and if you will allow people to read Christ in you, then you will see God bonding with you, and everyone will see God in you, around you, and that God is for you. The results will be like Joseph in his days—you shall be called a *prosperous person* because God will make all that you do to be prosperous, and it will be undeniable.

The fourth blessing is that you will find grace in the sight of your bosses, just as Joseph experienced in his days. You will be served by your bosses, and God will cause them to promote, and you will be accorded freedom that others will not enjoy because you are bonded with God. And because your bosses favoured you, God will bless them the more; this will become the circle of blessing for you and for your bosses, and as a result, you will become goodly and well favoured, even in the low ebbs where an ordinary person will never amount to anything.

CHAPTER 9

Temptation and Appearance of Evil

And it came to pass after these things, that his master's wife cast her eyes upon Joseph; and she said, lie with me. But he refused, and said unto his master's wife, Behold, my master wotteth not what is with me in the house, and he hath committed all that he hath to my hand; There is none greater in this house than I; neither hath he kept back any thing from me but thee, because thou art his wife: how then can I do this great wickedness and sin against God? And it came to pass, as she spake to Joseph day by day, that he hearkened not unto her, to lie by her, or to be with her. And it came to pass about this time, that Joseph went into the house to do his business; and there was none of the men of the house there within. And she caught him by his garment, saying, Lie with me: and he left his garment in her hand, and fled, and got him out. And it came to pass, when she saw that he had left his garment in her hand, and was fled forth.

—Genesis 39:7-13

This chapter started with "it came to pass after these things." The question, therefore, is "After what things?" The answer is not farfetched—it came to pass after the blessings that Joseph enjoyed as a result of God being with him and this seen by his boss, after Potiphar had promoted Joseph and given him the freedom and lifted him higher in his house, after Joseph had been made the head of all the slaves in the house of Potiphar, and after God had tremendously blessed Potiphar and his household because of Joseph; oh yes, it was after many years of Joseph lifting up the God of Abraham in the land of darkness and after Joseph had been radiating and shining the glory of God and preaching the God of truth to the dying world that Potiphar's wife cast her eyes on Joseph, asking him to commit adultery with her.

Son of God, you must be very careful of the danger in the time of ease. Be careful of the dangers that always lurk in waiting, particularly when you are celebrating the blessings of God. David—during the seasons when his life was in danger, from King Saul and from his son, Absalom—was on his guard 24-7 and always ready for battle, but when he had now fully taken over the throne that God promised him, when there seemed to be peace in all his surroundings, David went into peace mode even when the season for all kings to go to battle arrived, and David was busy flirting about on top of his roof with the evil of fornication that was lurking around the corner to prey on him.

I have seen several Christians that were previously strong for the Lord when they were going through challenging times: they were always in church for fellowship, they prayed regularly, and they studied the word of God; and as a result, God honoured his word in their life. Testimony followed them, and everyone could see that God had favoured them, but as soon as they entered into their time of abundance, they threw off all the spiritual principles; yes, they would not pray as before, they would not attend church regularly, and neither would they even remember to study the word of God and be the doers of the word.

They begin to live a life of compromise, their love for Master Jesus begins to wax cold, and they are unaware that just around the corner is the enemy of their soul. The Bible says in 1 Peter 5 verse 8 that "Be sober, be vigilant; because your adversary the devil, as a roaring lion, walketh about, and seeking whom he may devour." Rather than being sober (humble), they become arrogant and swell up with pride towards man and even against God, and as a result, they debase more and more into a reprobate mind-set, doing what is against the will of God.

But thank God for Joseph, a man who, in spite of the new privileges that was accorded him, was in touch with God and his word; hence, when the devil, the enemy of souls, struck through Zulaikha (Potiphar's wife), Joseph was not caught off guard. Oh yeah, Joseph knew that this was not Zulaikha but, rather, Satan trying to gain the position of glory that belonged to God. So also must you know that any sin you may be exposed to is from Satan, who always wants to take God's glory in your life.

When God created man in the book of Genesis, God expected man to serve him and obey him fully. God wanted every born-again sons of his to obey his words, irrespective of how many temptations and tests came their way. This Joseph realized and fully understood, so when the wife of Potiphar brought the sin of adultery to his door, he was able to resist her because this was more than just a sin against man but against God.

You cannot blame Potiphar's wife casting her eyes on Joseph; it was understandable, really, because Joseph was wearing God's glory and favour, and one thing with God's favour and glory is that they are warm, radiating, and they draw others. So also, children of God, understand that the grace, the favour, and the glory of God that surround you will attract others including unbelievers just as good food will attract flies and as flowers will always attract bees, but remember that if you allow the enemy of your soul to introduce sin into your life through the available "Potiphar's wife" of nowadays, you will certainly lose God, his favour, and his anointing upon your life.

Just like Joseph, every God's dream carrier must understand that the devil is interested not only in destroying you but also in causing miscarriages of the dreams of God inside of you. You must then be vigilant, ensuring that you do not fall a victim of his devices.

Also, let us consider it from another angle of understanding. One can stand to wonder and ask the one-million questions: "What did Potiphar's wife see in Joseph that made her so attracted to him when, after all, he was just a slave boy?" But the answer is not farfetched, for the Bible recorded that Joseph was a handsome young man, but was he so handsome, better than every other man in the land of Egypt. So why Joseph in particular? A theology historian even wrote that Potiphar's wife was a very chaste woman before this time, so what went wrong?

We must understand the simple principle of how the devil always operates since the time of the Garden of Eden. The devil always uses available tools to achieve his purpose. He used the serpent to deceive Eve and, in turn, used her to cause Adam to disobey God. If not for the vigilance of Christ, he also attempted using Peter to derail Jesus Christ from the perfect will of the heavenly Father. So also, it could be submitted that Potiphar's wife was just an available tool in the hands of Satan, whose aim was to get Joseph to sin against God. Brother and sister that are reading this book, be careful of the ones that Satan may use to cause you to derail; watch and pray!

Just like Joseph, be ready to refuse that gentile boss that casts his or her eyes on you and asks you to commit fornication and adultery with him or her. Be ready to refuse those links or mediums, those business opportunities that come with some sinful requirements and attachments; your falling for them will cause you to sin against God, the giver of dreams.

Note something very powerful in verse 8. The Bible recorded that Joseph gave reasons why he could not indulge himself in such evil act. The point here is, Joseph took time out to assess the situation, and he evaluated the situation through the eyes of the word of God. Just like David, Joseph was able to do this because he had taken time in the past to store in his heart the word of God, and when evil days came, the word became light unto his feet. Psalms 119:105.

Psalms 119:9 says, "Wherewithal shall a young man cleanse his way? By taking heed thereto according to thy word." It was very evident from the life of Joseph, even in prison, that he had been studying and meditating in the word of God day and night, just as Joshua was instructed to do in his days. Joshua 1:1-8. It is, therefore, my prayer to every reader of this book that God will make your desire to be in his word day and night.

The assessment of the situation by Joseph further confirmed that Joseph was a man that never leaned upon his own understanding; instead, he always acknowledged God who, in turn, ordered his steps. The offer of Potiphar's wife would have been very attractive to an ordinary young man of Joseph's age, but to Joseph, the friend of God, it was an evil act against God.

Are your thoughts always of the people you may hurt in the process of your selfish desires? When the adulterous woman or man come to your door, knocking with sweets and niceties that will never last, has it ever crossed your mind that your innocent partner's and family member's hearts will be broken?

More importantly, in this place is the thought of God in the heart of Joseph. In verse 8, Joseph saw the offer of Potiphar's wife as great wickedness and sinfulness against God. Why? Because Joseph had the fear of God in his heart; hence, he was a very wise man (Proverbs 9:10, 1:7). Oh yes, indeed, he was a very wise man. It takes wisdom to look further into the future and damn the opportunity and temporary enjoyment that will never last.

Joseph understood through God's wisdom that if he accepted Potiphar's wife's offer, in the meantime, he may enjoy some so-called fun, gifts, and high praise before Potiphar, but he certainly would lose the favour of God upon his life, he would lose the prosperity of God in his life, and he would have died a slave. So the best that Potiphar's wife could have given to him would have been enjoyed only in slavery; he would have remained a slave and died a slave.

My readers please do remember that anytime you act or will act unwisely and compromise your faith for any sinful and wicked act, though you may have some temporary satisfaction, which will never last forever, the downside is, you may have mortgaged your future, destiny, and greatness. It is very costly to accept the porridge offer of Jacob all because of temporary hunger; you may end up losing your birthright forever.

It is necessary to draw out to my reader that Joseph was a man that had been known to always stand for something; he stood for righteousness when he was at home with his family, and the Bible recorded that he would always report the evil acts of his brothers to their father. He, again, stood for godliness even in slavery, and he was, indeed, a voice for God even against the loud voice of his master's wife.

My reader, what do you stand for in your place of secular job? What does your neighbour know that you stand for in your neighbourhood, in your home, and among your friends and colleagues? Always remember that whoever refuses to stand for something will fall for everything. May the Lord help you to stand for God everywhere you go.

In verses 8 and 9, it could be noted that Joseph not only displayed integrity but he also equally displayed the spirit of faithfulness, loyalty to his boss, and dedication to his work. Joseph also showed that he was a grateful individual that appreciated all the benefits and kind gestures that he enjoyed from his boss, Potiphar. Will this be your testimony if your story is read aloud in many years to come?

Joseph equally acted in line with a good conscience when he drew to the attention of Potiphar's wife how grateful he was. Joseph also displayed godly wisdom here when he told Potiphar's wife that there was no gift that she would give to him that was not already placed in his care by her husband as a result of God's favour showered on him by God.

Children of God, will you show some godly wisdom whenever the enemy attempts to entice you with earthly blessings, which God has already given to you in the heavenly places through Christ Jesus as recorded in Ephesians 1:3? For the Bible says that nobody receives anything on earth except what has been given to him from above. John 3:27. Do not allow anyone or the devil himself to deceive you into believing that he can give you anything that God has not already called yours, which has been set to manifest in God's appointed time, only if you can trust, wait, and continue to believe God.

To everyone that has been pressurized, intimidated, and persecuted for doing the will of God and for standing against evil, I wish to encourage you to continue to stand for God, just as Joseph did while in the house of Potiphar. The Bible recorded in verse 10 that Potiphar's wife—day in, day out—pressurized Joseph. The intimidation was just much, and the persecution was very unbearable. All of a sudden, anything that Joseph did was not impressive anymore to Potiphar's wife, all because he refused to commit adultery with a woman that was not his wife.

It was so noticeable in Potiphar's house that something was not right between Madam Potiphar and the head slave; despite all this, Joseph remained calm in the Lord and continued to do his normal and daily duties. Joseph recognized that God, who had always been with him, would continue to be with him, providing he did not keep God away. In spite of the daily torments, Joseph stood firm on his integrity, and he held fast unto his belief in the God of Abraham. He refused to compromise his faith. Please, I beg you, no matter what the devil does to you, no matter how bad your financial affliction is, and no matter how difficult your challenges are, please do not compromise your faith in God, and do not deny the Lord Jesus Christ.

In verse 8, it was read that Joseph refused the free offer of Potiphar's wife because Joseph understood the principle of righteousness as laid down by God in his word. The Bible says in the book of 1 Thessalonians 5:22, "Flee from every appearance of sin." It means, "Abstain from all appearance of evil." Joseph started with a refusal of the demonic offer but ended up with fleeing, a sacrificial fleeing that cost him his garment, his employment, and his freedom.

Note that as God's dream carrier, fleeing from all appearances of evil on most occasions may cost you your garment, which may be your job, your family, your car, your financial stability, and just like Joseph, your freedom.

If Joseph had given in to the pressure of Potiphar's wife, he would have become one with her, and as one with an adulterous woman, a soul tie would be formed (1 Corinthians 6:16-18). Note this: Joseph becoming one with Potiphar's wife would have detached him from oneness with God and would have limited Joseph forever to the level of Potiphar's house, and given that Joseph's position in the house of Potiphar was a slave, Joseph would have died a slave.

Equally and according to the Bible in Proverbs 6:32, Joseph would have been seen by God as a man that lacked understanding, and as a result of his adultery, he would hurt his soul. Please do not commit adultery; it is a serious danger to your future. You will note that I only mention adultery, and you may, therefore, wonder why. It is because fornication, to my understanding, is the same as adultery.

Yes, I know that fornication is when two unmarried opposite sexes indulge in sexual immorality, but let me extend this definition of fornication in the light of adultery: Do you even consider that the unmarried lady or young man that you are committing sin with is actually somebody's wife or husband in the nearest future, and how would you feel if someone has defiled your future wife? You claim that you have plans to marry in future, but the point is, right now, you are not married, are you? How are you sure that this, your relationship of today, will lead to marriage in many years to come? Why don't you wait on God in trust for your future and, in the meantime, be one with God—stay chaste, stay unpolluted, and do not compromise.

But if I may ask you, is there anything too much to pay as a price for standing for Christ, for standing for your godly integrity, and for standing in the will of God? Remember, if you stand irrespective of the cost, it will work out for your good, for it is written in the word of God that everything works together for *good* to those that love God and that are called according to his purpose (Romans 8:28).

CHAPTER 10

God's Dreamer Falsely Accused

That she called unto the men of her house, and spake unto them, saying, See, he hath brought in an Hebrew unto us to mock us; he came in unto me to lie with me, and I cried with a loud voice. And it came to pass, when he heard that I lifted up my voice and cried, that he left his garment with me, and fled, and got him out. And she spake unto him according to these words, saying, The Hebrew servant, which thou hast brought unto us, came in unto me to mock me. And it came to pass, as I lifted up my voice and cried, that he left his garment with me, and fled out. And it came to pass, when his master heard the words of his wife, which she spake unto him, saying, After this manner did thy servant to me; that his wrath was kindled. And Joseph's master took him, and put him into the prison, a place where the king's prisoners were bound: and he was there in the prison.

—Genesis 39:14-20

The shame of the day for Joseph was too much and unimaginable. It may have been understandable and bearable if Joseph had, indeed, committed the attempted rape crime of which he had been accused of, but the fact that he was innocent made it more painful and difficult for Joseph to handle. The day started with Potiphar's wife drawing his cloth and asking for partnership in adultery, and then Joseph refused and fled and then came a cry of wolf and false accusation, and within minutes, Joseph was beaten till his bones were weak, all within a day—a sad happening to God's dream carrier.

One, therefore, stands to wonder if the dream of Joseph as ordained by God will ever come to pass. Right in front of Joseph was the offence charged with its long time prison. It would have been easy for Joseph if he was an Egyptian citizen with good connections; the matter may have been resolved in private. It may also have been easy if Joseph was charged to have attempted rape with an ordinary slave girl.

Maybe because of the love and respect that Potiphar had for him so far, judgment would have been tampered with mercy, but the fact remained that the accuser of Joseph was the wife of a highly placed officer of the king; hence, a slave boy with no family presence in the land of Egypt stood no chance without God. The situation looked so bleak, but God was all in it, and it was a journey in the right direction, and it must work for his good.

Somebody once asked what was God playing at to allow Joseph to be wrongly accused of a crime that may have cost him his life, but my answer to them was simple: God loves to complicate the challenges and multiply the situation so that when God steps in and provides a solution, it will become undeniably certain to all that this is the Lord's doing, and it then becomes marvellous in the sight of all.

The case of Joseph—who later became the prime minister of Egypt (the first and only civilised nation of the world at that time) with only one human vote (king/pharaoh)—is an undeniable testimony that God rules in the affairs of man and that he is the final-appeal judge in the kingdom of men.

Joseph's status could be described as, firstly, a foreigner in the land of Egypt; secondly, an ordinary slave boy in the common house of an officer of the state, called Potiphar; and lastly, a prisoner charged with attempted rape of the wife of a state official. And while in prison, to be pardoned and installed unopposed as the first prime minister of a very populated and the first civilised nation of the world is incredible but true, and there are records in the history of Egypt that Joseph was, indeed, the first prime minister of Egypt.

The God that did that for Joseph is still in charge and even more experienced in the field of making a "nobody" a ruler of many nations. However, the processes must be completed, for to everything under heaven, there are a time and a season. Just like Joseph, you must allow God's processes to complete fully, and while you are going through his ordained processes, ensure that you humble yourself under the mighty hand of God so that at his appointed time, he may lift you up.

In verse 14, Potiphar's wife called other Egyptian servants and lied to them that Joseph had attempted to rape her; she showed them the evidence of his cloth, and she even confessed that the arrival of Joseph in the house was an act of mockery. There were a ganging up and conspiracy going on against a man that was carrying God's dream.

A man of righteousness was now being set up for no just cause all because he made a choice to stand for God, and in all this, God did not intervene; oh yes, heaven was totally silent. Children of God, this may be where you are right now; you have been seriously persecuted for righteousness' sake, you have lost your good job and employment because you will not compromise your faith and stand in the Lord, and you have suffered in the hands of a man or a woman in marriage because you resolved to do it God's way. Oh, you were even accused of a crime that you knew nothing about, and throughout your ordeals, you felt abandoned by all, may be the devil even taunted you that you have been forsaken by God. I got good news for you: God has not forsaken you at all because He says in his word that He will never leave you nor forsake you; He also says again in His word that He will not give you more than what you can bear, and in all this, He will make a way of escape.

The Bible recorded that even Potiphar, that had seen God in Joseph and had been blessed because of Joseph, also believed his wife's lies, and he moved in anger and sent Joseph to prison. One can imagine what painful torture that Joseph went through on that day from the hand of Potiphar and his boys, but heaven kept silent; he must have been beaten, wounded, and terrified, but in all his painful experience, Joseph held on to his faith in the God of Abraham.

Joseph had reasons to murmur against God and accuse him of failing to act, humanly speaking, but he did not because he had an understanding that all things worked together for good to those that loved God and were called according to his purpose. You also must have the understanding that God will see to it that at the end of it all, it must work for your good.

God fully permitted Potiphar and his wife (human authority) to exercise their evil power, he allowed them to torture Joseph, and he even allowed them to send him into prison. At no point during these human injustices did God intervene even though he knew all things. Why? As far as God is concerned, the processes you go through do not really count, and what matters to him is that following the processes, you give birth to the dream of God inside of you.

The Bible explained the secret of God's plan about Joseph in the book of Psalms 105 from verses 17 onward. Therein, one can see that Joseph was just an integral part of the phases of the plan of God as he promised Abraham. The Bible said that God sent Joseph before them and he allowed him to be sold as a servant. Sons of God, in every challenge that you go through, remember that God has chosen you to go for him as his forerunner of great blessings yet to come.

So rejoice in your challenges; you are an appointed vessel of God, set to become a channel of blessing to those coming behind you. Whenever things are not the way they should be, whenever you are going through a very hard time, always remember that you were sent before. This, in the case of Joseph, caused him to suffer hard; he was laid in iron, and his foot was hurt with fetters. The Bible said in Psalms 105:19 that the word of the Lord tried him until the time that God's word came and Pharaoh set him free.

There is a revelation here, children of God. The first episode of the trial of Joseph was from men (people such as Potiphar and his wife); they enslaved Joseph, and they bruised him. The second episode was in verse 19: the word of God tried Joseph; yes, the word of God tried his patience, tried his level of perseverance and endurance until the time that God's word came unto fulfillment in Joseph's life.

Listen to me, sons of God, as God's dream carrier, it is always the case that you will go through several phases of persecution from people or circumstances, and time always passes before God's appointed time will come to pass, and within these times, God's word will test your heart, your patience, and your level of endurance. The Bible says in the book of James 1:4 to let patience fully have its full work in you so that you lack nothing.

So ensure that you do not fail the test put to you by God's word during your season of patience, for you shall laugh again. Lastly, I must draw your attention to the book of Psalms 66:10—12, which says, *"For thou, O God, hast proved us: thou hast tried us, as silver is tried. Thou brought us into the net; thou laid affliction upon our loins. Thou hast caused men to ride over our heads; we went through fire and through water: but thou brought us out into a wealthy place."* For if only you can trust God and follow the processes set by God before you, you shall, surely, soon enter into your wealthy place.

CHAPTER 11

God's Dreamer in the Underground (Prison)

And it came to pass, when his master heard the words of his wife, which she spake unto him, saying, After this manner did thy servant to me; that his wrath was kindled. And Joseph's master took him, and put him into the prison, a place where the king's prisoners were bound: and he was there in the prison. But the LORD was with Joseph, and shewed him mercy, and gave him favour in the sight of the keeper of the prison. And the keeper of the prison committed to Joseph's hand all the prisoners that were in the prison; and whatsoever they did there, he was the doer of it. The keeper of the prison looked not to any thing that was under his hand; because the LORD was with him, and that which he did, the LORD made it to prosper.

—Genesis 39:19-23

It may seem totally unthinkable, but sometimes, this is the way of the Lord—that a righteous man, who is carrying God's dream, has to be hidden in prison (underground) even though he is innocent of all accusations, and God keeps quiet.

Children of God, it is necessary to understand that God's ways are not our ways, and neither are his thought ours. Though God allowed Joseph to be taken down to prison without stopping the movement of the enemy, God ensured that Joseph was not sent to just any prison but to the right prison—the prison of the king.

When Potiphar was making his decision as to which prison he should send Joseph to, his thought was *I must send Joseph to a first-class prison where he will suffer hardest, and hence, I must send him to the king's prison.* But God said, "Yes, Potiphar, the king's prison is the only place Joseph must go." Indeed, the steps of the righteous are ordered by the Lord, and sometimes, the righteous may not even know it at first, but she or he will understand it by and by.

What is the prison that life has hidden you in without a justified reason, and what is the underground trap that you now find yourself in? Note that your prison that seems like your limitation today—your prison that seems to serve as a boxed room, and as a result, no one can see you from outside now—will one day become your comfort room and a good, lasting memory.

What is a prison? A prison is any confinement where challenges have hidden you. Are you a minister of the gospel, and have you been in the ministry for many years, growing the ministry in the confinement or underground where you are hidden? I have news for you: it is for a good purpose, and it will work out for your good.

An underground is a place far under the soil. In the Western world, there are several modes of transportation, and one of them is called the underground train station. The trains run under the ground, and they are never seen on the surface; and for anyone to travel in them, you have to descend lower to board the underground train. During the underground travelling, travellers will not be seen on the surface for the duration of their journey. But once they get to the ending of their journey, they will come out at the other end, settled and refreshed.

There are observations I wish to draw out in the scenario illustrated above. Everyone loves to travel, for several reasons, on the surface, such as in the comfort of their own car, but the problem mostly is that there is huge traffic on the surface; hence, the journey will always take anyone longer to get to their expected destinations.

But when you have forgone the luxury of a car and boarded the underground train, though you will not be seen for a while on the surface, though there may be little or no comfort in the underground train, though the train may be so crowded during the rush hours, though there is limited or no good views underground, and though you may not be in charge of the train and your stays in the carriages of the train are directed and driven by another—either by a train driver or via a remote-control room located somewhere else, however, it is undeniable that you are more than likely to arrive at your destination quicker, sooner, and more refreshing than someone who has decided to travel in the comfort of their car, via a traffic-congested road.

So also in your situation, friends, God may allow you to be taken through prison of life; this may include some life limitations like the lack of money to carry out the dreams in your heart, this may include underground of limitations and austerity measures for a while, this may also include a phase of sickness or a wilderness of loneliness. But I have news for you: God has a plan for you, and the plan is made clear in the book of Jeremiah 29:11: *"For I know the plans I have concerning you, to give you a future and something to hope for."* And if I may add this also—God's plans are not only to give you a future and a hope but also to bring you into it faster than others who have been running wild in their "surface car" and in congested traffic.

You know what? By the time you come out at the other side and you look back, you will discover that everyone that started the journey before or at the same time as you but relied on their own understanding will be always behind you. They will always look at you ahead of them, and they will begin to wonder how you got there before them.

However, there are prices to pay while you are underground in the prison of life. While you are there, your movement will become restricted and limited. Every step you attempt to take leads to nowhere, and you are like back to square one. When you attempt to embark on ideas, dreams, and visions that are lurking inside of you, you will discover that things are not happening, but remember, this is God's dreamer in the underground prison of life and that God has a plan.

In the prison or underground of life, you will discover that you are not in control. Others that you will never have submitted to, all things being equal, will now be lords over you. Oh, ordinary people will work all over you, and you may be even cheated of what belongs to you and denied of your right, but always remember that God is always in control and he will work it for your good.

There were three things that Joseph suffered during his own underground trials: firstly, Joseph was forcefully taken without his consent; secondly, he was thrown into the prison of the king; and lastly, he was kept in bondage. His freedom was restricted even in a closed prison, but the Bible recorded in chapter 39:21 that God was with him.

Whoa! When Joseph was thrown into the prison, God too volunteered to enter into the prison with him. One would think that God would rather prefer to rescue Joseph from going to prison, but instead, God did not stop the activity of man towards his dream carrier; rather, he too entered the prison with Joseph.

I can imagine God saying to Joseph, "Don't worry, son, we are going into the prison together." That explained why Joseph was not moved or worried, even with all the challenges that he went through. Children of God understand that even in the underground you are currently in or you are just about to face, God is with you to provide you comfort and favour. Jesus says in the book of John that he will not leave you without a helper but that he will send you the Holy Spirit, the comforter, who shall teach you all truth.

The Bible said that God was with Joseph even in prison; the prison of the king received an unusual visitor. God became a resident of the king's prison because his dream carrier was locked in there; but was God just passively in prison with Joseph? Not at all; verse 21 said that God was in the prison, showing Joseph mercy and favour in the sight of the keeper of the prison.

Remember that Joseph entered the prison under difficult conditions; he was bound, and I believe that Potiphar would have given instructions to the keeper of the prison to ensure that Joseph was severely punished for the untrue charge of attempted rape, but God who owned the heart of the king and, like a flowing river, directed it into where he wanted—entered into the heart of the keeper of the prison and began to release his mercy and favour into it towards Joseph.

May the heavenly Father release mercy and favour upon you today so that you will find favour in the eyes of your captors, in Jesus' name. (Amen.)

God's intervention on behalf of Joseph, first and foremost, drew him to the attention of the keeper of the prison, and all of a sudden, Joseph became noticed and wanted; he became the star of the prison for no particular thing he had done that made him outshine others who got there before him.

Have in your mind that the prison of the king is mainly for movers and shakers of Egypt whom the king cast therein for punishment, confinement, and in some cases, execution; hence, ordinary people do not go to the prison of the king except when you are rich and famous and a citizen of the soil. But for a foreigner with a slave status and, worse still, thrown in prison for a rape-related matter, and now have found favour in the eyes of the keeper of the prison could only be God's work.

Note that God did not get Joseph out of the prison, and neither did the mercy and favour of God that Joseph found in the prison keeper's eyes persuade the keeper to release Joseph. The purpose of the mercy and the favour was only, at this stage, to relax the harsh condition that Joseph was placed in the prison. Just like for Joseph, it may be the situation sometimes that the favour and mercy of God that you will enjoy in the eyes of your bosses, employers, and anyone may not free you right away from the challenges you are going through, but they will give you freedom and peace until God's set time for your freedom will come.

The result of God's presence in the prison and his providing mercy and favour for Joseph to enjoy became so evidential within a very short time of being cast into prison. Verses 22-23 recorded that, consequently, the keeper of the prison committed to Joseph's hand all the prisoners that were in the prison; and whatsoever they did there, the Bible said that Joseph was the doer of it. It was recorded also that the keeper of the prison looked not to anything that was under his hand because the Lord was with him, and God made prosper all that he did, even in prison! Certainly, this was not the intention of Potiphar and his wife when they cast Joseph into the king's prison.

Their plan was to make him suffer until he would gradually waste away, but what they failed to understand was that whenever any of God's dream carriers is cast into prison or a difficult and challenging situation, God is always there. This is because part of God, or better still, God himself is right inside the dream carrier and whenever God entered into the difficult situation, He always thwart the plan of the enemy and even make difficult and challenging situation to become a ground of ease.

Oh yes, he is the God that makes Nebuchadnezzar's fire to become a cool and peaceful conference center for the three Hebrews, and he is the same God that turns a lion's den into a resting bedroom for Daniel. May he enter your hard times with you and turn your hostile enemy to become your friend. May he grant you favour and mercy in the face of man's severe judgment.

The Bible says that if the ways of a man please the Lord, he will make even his enemies to become his friends. Proverbs 16:7. Joseph's ways pleased the Lord; hence, he caused the keeper of the prison to become his pal. For a man that was cast into prison in bounds and following God showing favour and mercy, the story changed; suddenly, his chains were loosened, he was allowed to move freely within the prison, and he was promoted to the position of assistant governor of the prison.

A foreigner, slave boy, and accused criminal in the king's prison giving orders to executives of the land of Egypt—this can only be the Lord's doing. Within a short period, the story changed. In the prison, all inmates were informed, "If you need anything right here, speak to Mr. Joseph Israel, the Hebrew boy, because he is in charge." May the good Lord of mercy and favour show you favour and mercy today in any situation you are currently going through. May mercy and favour promote you and lift you higher, and may they preserve you and give you peace that surpasses all human understanding, in the name of the Lord Jesus Christ. (Say a louder *amen*.)

James 2:13 said that mercy prevailed over judgment; God realized that Joseph had been judged by evil men and women who had perverse justice, so God understood that judgment was about punishment and unless he (God) brought mercy into Joseph's situation, there was no hope for him. So God introduced his mercy into the judgment of man passed upon Joseph, and consequently, God's mercy prevailed over man's judgment. May the mercy of God be introduced by the almighty God into your situation today, in the name of the Lord Jesus.

One thing about mercy is that no one deserves it, and right inside of mercy or side by side with mercy is the favour of God. Oh yes, mercy means "unmerited favour," so God sends his mercy and favour (twin brothers) to overrule the judgment that men think Joseph deserves. Yes, they pass judgment on you today, and judgment of lies has been passed on some readers; everywhere you go, somebody spreads lies about you, and they just wish to discredit your image, and may the mercy and favour of God prevail over all lying judgments and lying tongues of the enemy, in the name of Jesus Christ.

Lastly, on this chapter, you must understand that mercy and favour brought fresh air even in prison (a difficult and hard place), the mercy and favour of God brought freedom from bondage, and the favour and mercy of God brought promotion and made a mere slave to become known in a strange land—prison.

Do you know, my reader that it does not matter where life has cast you and it does not matter, under any circumstances, that life has hidden you. When God's favour and mercy prevail over the judgment of the enemy that has held you bound, promotion will follow; even in the situation, you will have the ability and right to manage. Oh yes, you will be on top. Right now, I can feel the anointing of the Lord all over you, so why don't you just turn it into prayer wherever you are right now? "Oh Lord, please send into my situation your mercy and favour so that they prevail over every judgment of the enemy today, in Jesus Christ's name."

CHAPTER 12

Hidden but Not Forgotten

And it came to pass after these things, that the butler of the king of Egypt and his baker had offended their lord the king of Egypt. And Pharaoh was wroth against two of his officers, against the chief of the butlers, and against the chief of the bakers. And he put them in ward in the house of the captain of the guard, into the prison, the place where Joseph was bound. And the captain of the guard charged Joseph with them, and he served them: and they continued a season in ward. And they dreamed a dream both of them, each man his dream in one night, each man according to the interpretation of his dream, the butler and the baker of the king of Egypt, which were bound in the prison. And Joseph came in unto them in the morning, and looked upon them, and, behold, they were sad. And he asked Pharaoh's officers that were with him in the ward of his lord's house, saying, Wherefore look ye so sadly to day? And they said unto him, We have dreamed a dream, and there is no interpreter of it. And Joseph said unto

> *them, Do not interpretations belong to God? tell me*
> *them, I pray you.*

—Genesis 40:1-8

There is something that runs across this story of Joseph, and that is the phrase "It came to pass after these things." When you look at Genesis 39:7 and several verses therein; you will note that the above phrase is regularly used. So also again, the same phrase is used in chapter 40:1. Why? This denotes the ending of a situation and the beginning of another phase. Friends, please understand that whatsoever you are currently going through will not last forever—that, I hope, will be a consolation for somebody that is going through a very challenging season right now in their destiny.

The Bible says in Ecclesiastes 3:1 that there are time and season for everything under heaven, and the good news is that God has set times and seasons. So let no enemy take the glory that belongs to God. Whenever the devil comes with his thoughts right inside of your mind, remember that he is a liar and the father of lies. He is not in charge of time and season, and he does not have a clue of what is around the corner for your life, but God does. In the book of Isaiah 42:9, God rightly claimed that he predicted the old things and they came to pass, and now, he is predicting a new thing that shall spring forth.

The devil has no clue about your tomorrow—that explains why he hangs on to your today's challenges and also wants you to continue to focus on your today's challenges so that you will not see the new things that God has done and now brings to you in your tomorrow. Please, friends, open your eyes and see—behold—for as far as you can see (into the future, into your tomorrow), God says that he has already given to you.

"It came to pass after these things." Friends, until some things come to pass in your life, the next level will not happen. Oh yes, please do not run away from something all because it is not sweet or because it is not palatable. Even Jesus says to John the Baptist in Matthew 3:15 that things that have been written must be fulfilled or come to pass. Yes, I know that they are difficult, hard, and challenging, but they are inevitably necessary, and if you truly understand the processes of God, you will know that *all things truly work together.*

For these things to come to pass, just like in the life of Joseph, you have to allow patience and endurance to have their full work in you so that you may lack nothing. Right now, you feel like you are going through a dark night time; don't worry, trust in God, spend time in his word, and always pray and follow the leading of the Holy Spirit. It will work itself out for your good. Though the sorrow tarries all night, the Bible says, joy cometh in the morning (tell yourself, "Be patient, it will work itself out for your good.")

A word of warning for all that are currently enjoying a season of celebration and wonderful testimonies of the goodness of God—you must also know that this season will not last forever, for there will always be wilderness right in front of you pretty soon as ordained by God, not to destroy you, but to test you further, and following every test, there is a promotion.

The Bible said in the book of Matthew 4:1 that immediately after the public manifestation of the Lord Jesus Christ to the public, he was led into the wilderness by the Holy Spirit to be tested. Jesus was not even given the chance to enjoy his newly found fame and honour before being led into the next phase of his life, but do you realise that following the testing of our Lord Jesus Christ, his ministry took off into another level. Get ready for some new things coming to pass after all these things.

Though Joseph was hidden, he was not forgotten; delay was not denial. That God has allowed life and its challenges to hide you away or that you have been serving God all this while in difficult circumstances, you have prayed so hard, you have faith all through, you have even made so many confessions, but still, the members that God has promised you many years ago are yet to come along.

Oh, yesterday, you had dreams of a packed church with wonderful choir members, but when you woke up, you were still stocked with the reality of three to ten members in your services. Great men and women of God had prophesied of what God had in stock for your life over many years ago, but even as you read this book, you have no job, no family of your own.

You have seen yourself carrying children in visions and dreams, but as we speak, you have not even one child in your home even after twenty years in marriage. I have great news for you as a prophet of the living God: the heavenly Father of our Lord Jesus Christ has a big plan for you, and you may be hidden right now, but remember that you are not forgotten, and delay is not denial; you shall smile again.

When evil men came to the end of their evil plot, then God's plans would come to play. Right here in the case of Joseph, the Bible recorded that two officers of the king offended the king, and the king cast them into the prison. When God wants to bless his own, he will even cause another to step out of line in order to create a level, plane field for his own.

The two officers of the king became prison mates of Joseph all because God was about to promote his own. Yes, bad people and life hid Joseph in the prison of the king, but God knew about it; Joseph did not fight for himself, but he submitted himself into the hands of the heavenly God, who was the right judge in all circumstances.

And since he can trust God enough to handle things for him in his own way and time, God too returns to prove to Joseph that he is the king of the chess game.

First, he gave Joseph mercy and favour that prevailed over the judgment of man in Joseph's life; second, he gave him favour that created his freedom, even in a supposed prison; third, he now brought down two officers of the king into the same prison where Joseph was kept and given the right of rulership—God's aim was to bring Joseph into contact and relationship with the king's officers, who would eventually become Joseph's link to the king in many years to come.

God always has a perfect plan on how to bring you into a wealthy place, but many times, the plans may seem long, foolish, and unthinkable, but the foolishness of God is wiser than the wisdom of man. He is God in all dimensions.

Joseph was hidden but not forgotten at all. Although Potiphar's household had totally forgotten about him, as far as they were concerned, Joseph was history. His brothers had also forgotten about him; after all, they lied to their father that a wild animal killed him, so as far as everyone was concerned, Joseph was either dead or dying daily and gradually, but as far as heaven was concerned, Joseph was into a new life.

Oh Lord, Joseph may have, indeed, died to the outside world in fulfilment of the word of God that says that except the seed that falls to the ground and dies, it abideth alone, but when it dies, it brings forth new life.

This may be you right here, friends, and people think that it is over for you and that they have got you where they want you, but they have forgotten something very important, for all things shall work together for your good because you love God and you are called for his purpose. God so much orchestrated the moves of this officer that he ensured not only that they were kept in the same prison with Joseph but also that they were handed over to the same captain of the guard who was in charge of Joseph. Why divine connection? It was not a coincidence or accident; it was the perfect plan of God.

I, therefore, encourage you to please begin to let go and let God do what he is best known to do in your life. Let him work out the modality of your future; he is a pro, and you can trust him. Just like Joseph, you may not understand why things are moving so fast and how they move, but rest assured your heavenly Father is in control.

The Bible recorded that the guard charged Joseph with them and Joseph served them. Joseph was given a task in the prison, and he was humble enough to discharge his daily duties with the fear of God. Joseph remembered the word of God that said that in all that you find in doing, do it as if unto the Lord. So Joseph served the two officers, and he looked after their well-being not for any favours expected in return but for service unto the Lord. Oh yes, Joseph had a servant's hands, and he did everything in his service to make God happy.

What about you, child of God? Do you have a servant's heart, and do you do anything and everything as if unto the Lord, or do you only do things for financial gain? In your secular place of work, are you malingering and skipping office, going sick every day even when you are not sick? Whenever you do attend your office, do you get there on time, or are you always late? And whenever you arrive late, do you lie about your time sheet?

Joseph was doing his daily work with one thing in his mind: *I must please God.* Joseph would never take advantage of his employer, he would not steal the employer's time for personal use, and he would not steal his employer's pencils, pens, papers, and other office stationery that he was not given permission to have for his family use; can you become another Joseph?

Joseph was not even trying to manipulate the officers, because of their close position to the king, to secure his freedom; rather, he put his trust in the God of heaven that started his journey and that must finish it and take all the glory. Whom are you looking up to for your financial independence and freedom, your employers, bosses? How wrong you would be if you did everything this way. Why don't you join David, in the book of Psalms 121, who says that *"I will look up to the hills where cometh my help, and my help comes from the Lord, who made heaven and the earth."*

CHAPTER 13

The Gift of the Righteous Makes Room

And the chief butler told his dream to Joseph, and said to him, In my dream, behold, a vine was before me; And in the vine were three branches: and it was as though it budded, and her blossoms shot forth; and the clusters thereof brought forth ripe grapes: And Pharaoh's cup was in my hand: and I took the grapes, and pressed them into Pharaoh's cup, and I gave the cup into Pharaoh's hand. And Joseph said unto him, This is the interpretation of it: The three branches are three days: Yet within three days shall Pharaoh lift up thine head, and restore thee unto thy place: and thou shalt deliver Pharaoh's cup into his hand, after the former manner when thou wast his butler. But think on me when it shall be well with thee, and shew kindness, I pray thee, unto me, and make mention of me unto Pharaoh, and bring me out of this house: For indeed I was stolen away out of the land of the Hebrews: and here also have I done nothing that they should put me into the dungeon. When the chief baker saw that the interpretation was good, he said unto Joseph, I also was in my dream, and, behold, I had three white baskets on my head: And in the uppermost basket there was of all manner of bake meats for Pharaoh; and the birds did eat them out of the basket upon my head. And Joseph answered and said, This is the interpretation thereof: The three baskets are three days: Yet within three days shall Pharaoh lift up thy head from off thee, and shall hang thee on a tree; and the birds shall eat thy flesh from off thee. And it came to pass the third day, which was Pharaoh's birthday, that he made a feast unto all his servants: and he lifted up the head of the chief butler and of the chief baker among his servants. And he restored the chief butler unto his butlership again; and he gave the cup into Pharaoh's hand: But he hanged the chief baker: as Joseph had interpreted to them. Yet did not the chief butler remember Joseph, but forgat him.

—Genesis 40:9-23

Here, again, we see a man that is pregnant with God's dream, more concerned, maybe, with helping and rendering godly services to those that are in need. In spite of the situation and challenges that Joseph found himself in, rather than concentrating on his sad situation and false imprisonment, instead of allowing a bleak and uncertain future to cause him to be more preoccupied with grief, pain, and sorrow, he allowed his God-given gift to, first, make a room for him among the prisoners of the king's prison and, secondly, rise to the occasion of using his gift of interpretation of dreams to help the helpless.

So also, children of God, irrespective of the difficult situations and challenges you are currently undergoing, the hard times and trials you experience do not matter; make sure that you allow your God-given gifts to come to play and assist others. Are you looking for the fruit of the womb? Let me let you in a secret of God in this area. Look for another person who is seeking the face of God for a child, and just like Joseph, begin to intercede for them before God, and pray that God will give the fruit of the womb. I can assure you as a prophet of the Lord in this end-time that as you begin to do this for another with a sincere heart, as you continue to use your gift of intercession to assist someone else's need through your prayer, the good God will also answer you.

I heard of a woman that had been seeking God's face for a very long time for the fruit of the womb. One day, the Lord told her to stop praying for herself but to look for another person that was seeking a baby and begin to pray for her need.

The woman obeyed God and began to pray for another woman that was seeking the fruit of the womb. She prayed so hard from a compassionate heart, given that she was in the same state. She understood what the other woman was going through because she was right there; hence, her prayers for her were also for herself as far as God was concerned. Not too long thereafter, God answered her prayer for the other lady, who became pregnant, and in the same month, she too discovered that she was pregnant, all because she interceded for the other woman.

It could be seen in verse 14 to 15 of this chapter that Joseph immediately introduced himself to the cupbearer, and he told him of his predicament and his innocence. Friends, Joseph has the wisdom of God; hence, he knows the time (his time) and what he ought to be doing. Joseph saw his chance and opportunity, and he was ready to grab it. Joseph knows that time and chance happen to all. Ecclesiastes 9:12.

Friends, when you see your opportunity, how do you react to it? So many people are not ready when their opportunity comes, some are too shy and timid, while some are unprepared, and in most cases, opportunity only comes but once.

Many have abused their God-ordained opportunities while many have treated them with levity. Do you know that in life, you do not need money to succeed? All you need is God's favour, and how does God send his favour? He sends favour through fellow men and women that he sends into your life. When you identify them in your season and you treat them with respect, you are, therefore, strategically positioned to receive God's favour through them.

Some of us are so secretive to the extent that even when God orders our steps to come across our helpers just like Joseph did, we are not able or willing to reach up to them and receive God's predestined blessing. Because of pride and arrogance of heart, so many find it too difficult to humble themselves even when they are so close to their God-ordained favour. But in the situation of Joseph, he was humbled enough to receive and be so willing and ready to request for help; in fact, Joseph was so specific as to what he wanted—freedom. This is godly wisdom; may that grace come over you as you read this book, in Jesus name.

To show that Joseph was not taking advantage of the good time expectation from the cupbearer but was rather a man with a heart of service, he, in verses 16 to 19 of this chapter, provided equal assistance even to the head baker. Joseph took his time, just like with the cupbearer, to hear out the dream of the head baker; following which he interpreted the baker's dream sincerely and with godly integrity.

It would not be an understatement to conclude that, as a result of Joseph's regular usage of his gift to praise and glorify God and to serve humanity, God ensured that every word (interpretation) of Joseph to the two men came to pass just as Joseph said it would; hence, this confirmed that Joseph was a prophet of the living God in the service of humanity.

A dreamer boy—who grew in righteousness and in the knowledge of God's word, notwithstanding his challenges—became a prophet of God, with words that always came to pass; what a promotion. Do you know, my friend, that if you can make use of your God-given gift to serve man unto God, irrespective of your challenges, and you continue to grow in God's righteousness, I can assure you that God will promote you.

This chapter will not be complete without a few revelations on verse 23. The Bible stated that even though everything that prophet Joseph said in his interpretations of the men's dreams came to pass and in spite of the promise and undertaking given to Joseph by the cupbearer that he will table his matter before the king upon his release, it is sad to note that the cupbearer did not remember Joseph.

Are you the type of person that promises but fails to honour it? You make several pledges to others, but you have not redeemed even one; you even make several vows unto the Lord in the time of your need, but now that God has answered, you have forgotten all about it! Whoa, what a bad way to live life. Amend your ways today, for the Bible says that let your *yes* be *yes* and your *no* be *no*; anything outside of this is evil. The Bible also says that you must not make foolish vows, and when you make one, ensure that you redeem your vows as failure to do so will always attract fatal consequences. Ecclesiastes 5:4 and Matthew 5:37.

Friends, please understand that there is no man or woman that can assist you or provide solution to your problem unless and except when God allows them to do so and in his set time. Why, you may ask? He will not share his glory with anyone; he is God. I will, therefore, encourage you, please do not put your hope in anyone. Yes, you should seek for assistance, but ensure that your steps are being ordered by the Lord. Just like Joseph, he was led to seek assistance from the cupbearer; however, his trust was in the God of Abraham, Isaac, and Jacob. That explained why he was not too disappointed when the mere man let him down. Psalms 146:3, Psalms 118:8, and Hosea 10:13-14.

CHAPTER 14

God's Unknown Agenda

Yet did not the chief Butler remember Joseph, but forgot him.

—Genesis 40:23

And it came to pass at the end of two full years that Pharaoh dreamed: and, behold, he stood by the river. And, behold, there came up out of the river seven well favoured kine and fat fleshed; and they fed in a meadow. And, behold, seven other kine came up after them out of the river, ill favoured and lean fleshed; and stood by the other kine upon the brink of the river. And the ill favoured and lean fleshed kine did eat up the seven well favoured and fat kine. So Pharaoh awoke. And he slept and dreamed the second time: and, behold, seven ears of corn came up upon one stalk, rank and good. And, behold seven thin ears and blasted with the east wind sprung up after them. And the seven thin ears

> *devoured the seven rank and full ears. And Pharaoh*
> *awoke, and, behold, it was a dream.*

—Genesis 41:1-7

The Bible started in Genesis 40:23 with the phrase *"Yet did not the chief Butler remember Joseph, but forgot him."* However, it is imperative to understand that though the chief butler may not have remembered Joseph and, in fact, for another two years, God has not forgotten Joseph, and neither has God stopped his plan for his life. Jeremiah 29:11 says that *"For I know the plans that I have concerning you, the plans to give you a future and something to hope."*

So while Joseph would have humanly thought that *Whoa, freedom is very near at last*, he never knew that another two years would go by before his expected freedom would come. Notwithstanding the waiting and what could be termed as disappointment but a blessing in disguise, Joseph hoped, trusted, and had faith in the God of Abraham, Isaac, and Israel did not fail. I, therefore, encourage you, my reader, that you must understand that irrespective of disappointed promises and letdowns, the promises of God shall surely stand.

You may not know why God allowed you to come across what you initially saw as God's appointment, and you may not also understand why what you previously saw as God's opened door, all of a sudden, became a disappointment and closed door; however, in all things, the Bible instructs you to give thanks and trust him that can do all things, and in due time, you will understand that God always has a good hidden agenda, and it will work out for your good. Can you say a louder *amen*?

It is very necessary to point out to you that despite the failed promises that Joseph went through for another two years, Joseph continued to be God's man even in the prison of challenges. One would expect negative reactions and behaviours from a man that had suffered disappointment from a dignitary such as the king's chief butler who promised and failed; rather, Joseph was calm, joyous, and active in the day-to-day responsibilities, which was committed into his hands in the prison.

My reader, how do you handle or react to disappointments whenever they come your way? Yes, I understand that your fiancée or fiancé has just jilted you. Oh yes, I can see that your husband or wife has left you for another woman or, in some worse scenario, for a man. As much as all these may be so bad, but let me ask you these very questions: "How do you react to the situation? Do you respond to it with a heart of thanksgiving and trust in the almighty God, or do you blame yourself and every other person around you for the situation? Do you continue to wallow in self-pity? Do you stop loving and start shutting everyone out of your life? Do you stop reading the word of God, attending fellowship, and praying, or have you altogether quit church and begun to walk in unforgiving?"

Joseph, in his time, handled it differently; he was disappointed, humanly speaking, but he refused to allow the disappointment to shut God out of his life. His disappointment, rather than taking him farther away from God, actually drew him closer unto him.

Readers, two good years went by before God's next move came to play. In Genesis 41:1, it became apparent that the fire of relationship between Joseph and the chief butler, which one would think to have grown into Joseph's freedom, had actually suffered a setback for another two years, a no-show; however, God had an agenda.

Do you know that God has an agenda for your life? With that child of yours that you have prayed for to return to Christ for so many years but have continued to create disappointment and embarrassment to you, I have got good news for you: God has a good agenda. You may not understand his plans and his ways of doing things, but God has a good agenda for you.

God's agenda now began to come to play in God's appointed time, from Genesis 41:1-7. You will note that following a complete circle of two full years, Pharaoh dreamt twice. No one knows why he was programmed with two significant dreams after years, but there could be no doubt in the heart of anyone that the dreams were no ordinary dreams but God's agenda coming to play.

Readers, there are agendas in the heart of God for you, and these good agendas have been programmed to play in God's set timing. It is, therefore, my prayer that God of heaven, in the name of the Lord Jesus Christ, will strengthen you with patience and endurance to wait and tarry in his presence and his rest until the set time of God.

Lastly on this, God, without discussing any of his plans of freedom with Joseph, began to set up the number 1 man of the land. Pharaoh, for two consecutive nights, was disturbed and troubled so that Joseph can be released and enthroned into the office that had never been in existence before then, and all this was happening without Joseph's knowledge of it. May I encourage someone to please continue to serve God without further complaints, for God is working on his good hidden agenda for your life. Listen to this, somebody: right now as you are reading this book, God is troubling someone in a high position of authority and influence to bless you. Say a big *amen*!

Without dwelling any further or going into the dreams of Pharaoh, we must understand that you have the answer to the riddles of another man that God has ordained to bless and promote you. The answer to the dreams that troubled Pharaoh was right in the prison, behind bars, for a crime for which he had been sentenced to a life imprisonment.

But without the solution from Joseph's mouth, Pharaoh's dreams would continue to be his nightmares, and they continued to bug his mind. It is, therefore, the only option to, first, release and give state pardon to Joseph before he (the king) can get his own freedom from the prison of the dreams that have now captivated him. You are the solution to an important person's challenges, so get ready; your freedom is very much closer than you ever thought.

Lastly on this point, you must know that Joseph had periods in his challenges, starting from the moment he had his dreams, and they were all to prepare him for the future when he would be standing before the king of Egypt. When Joseph had completed and passed his test in the classroom of conceiving and sharing his dreams, he was promoted into the classroom of the interpretation of dreams of ordinary men (such as the chief butler) without any rewards from them, but when he continued to focus on serving God even in his challenging circumstances, he was promoted by God to the stand before kings, and his developed gifts made his room before kings, and so shall it be for you, in Jesus' name!

CHAPTER 15

Invisible God Working Behind the Scene

Now it came to pass in the morning that his spirit was troubled, and he sent and called for all the magicians of Egypt and all its wise men. And Pharaoh told them his dreams, but there was no one who could interpret them for Pharaoh. Then the chief butler spoke to Pharaoh, saying: "I remember my faults this day. When Pharaoh was angry with his servants, and put me in custody in the house of the captain of the guard, both me and the chief baker, we each had a dream in one night, he and I. Each of us dreamed according to the interpretation of his own dream. Now there was a young Hebrew man with us there, a servant of the captain of the guard. And we told him, and he interpreted our dreams for us; to each man he interpreted according to his own dream. And it came to pass, just as he interpreted for us, so it happened. He restored me to my office, and he hanged him."

—Genesis 41:8-13

We are serving an invisible God that always works behind the scenes. That explains why the whole people of Egypt (that including Pharaoh himself) could not refuse to give all their gold and silver over to the people of Israel. Why? Because the invisible hand of God was behind the scene.

The Bible said in the above verses that it came to pass. Do you remember that the book of Habakkuk 2:3 says that it will surely come to pass? So also will it be in your life; a day will come when all that God has spoken about you and concerning you will come to pass.

Note the following when God's set time comes to pass; things will begin to move smoothly as he planned it, even without your involvement and realisation. The spirit of Pharaoh was troubled all because God's invisible hand was working behind the scene. The Bible says that the heart of the king is in God's hands, and he directs them as a flowing river to wherever chosen. So God stirred the spirit of Pharaoh with dreams whose solution was hidden in the hands of Joseph. The Bible said that Pharaoh called all his magicians, seeking assistance from those that God had not ordained to assist him.

The dreams that troubled Pharaoh were not ordinary dreams but ones sent by God; hence, only God's men had the solution to it. Do you know that it does not matter, even if Pharaoh does not know it yet, that his solution to his challenges (dreams) was in the hands of Joseph, a man hidden in his prison? However, the invisible hand of God that started the work would continue to work until the work was completed to the full.

While the troubles of Pharaoh continued to compound and no solutions were forthcoming from his expected sources of hope, the invisible hand of God came into play again. All of a sudden, after two full years had passed on, the chief butler's memory was touched and reactivated by God.

He remembered his faults; what faults? The faults of making a pledge to Joseph and forgetting to remember and aid his freedom. But he could not provide any help unless and until God enabled him, for God's glory would never be shared by any man. Maybe that is the reason why those that promised you have not yet remembered you. This is my word of encouragement to you, dear friend: continue to trust God and look only to him for help, for except when God builds the house, the labourer labours in vain, and except when God watches the city, the watcher watches in vain.

The invisible hand of God caused the chief butler to speak forth on behalf of a forgotten lad that had suffered injustice. Who knows? Maybe you are currently reading this book right inside of a prison, and you have been locked away as a result of the miscarriage of justice; I mean, you were framed up. I have got news for you—God's invisible hand will work behind the scene, and even your chief butler will begin to speak forth for your release as the Lord of heaven will trouble your pharaoh.

Given that the invisible hand of God now worked in the palace of Pharaoh on behalf of Joseph (a lad that was not even aware that God was working out his freedom), the chief butler began to advertise Joseph to the king as the only viable solution and that he could interpret his dreams. He narrated to the king the qualities that Joseph possessed, such as being an interpreter of dreams, a man of good and happy nature that continued to serve others even in difficult circumstances.

He referred to Joseph as not only a Hebrew boy but also a servant of the prison guard. This speaks volume about the qualities of Joseph. What the chief butler was saying here was that for a foreigner (a Hebrew man from a faraway land) to now get appointed by the captain of the king's guard, there must have been seen in him huge treasures and values.

The invisible hand of the Lord, working on behalf of Joseph, carefully selected the right words that would capture the heart of the king towards a Hebrew prisoner that had not been seen by the king. One can imagine the king saying, "Whoa, if this lad is this good, why has he being wasting away in my prison all this while? I need him right now because I need urgent help." I, therefore declare as a prophet of God upon you, that right now as you read this treasure book, may the invisible hand of God that worked for Joseph, begin to work for you, in Jesus name.

Chapter 16

The Test of a Dreamer — A Day Long Awaited

Then Pharaoh sent and called Joseph, and they brought him quickly out of the dungeon; and he shaved, changed his clothing, and came to Pharaoh. And Pharaoh said to Joseph, "I have had a dream, and there is no one who can interpret it. But I have heard it said of you that you can understand a dream, to interpret it." So Joseph answered Pharaoh, saying, "It is not in me; God will give Pharaoh an answer of peace." Then Pharaoh said to Joseph: "Behold, in my dream I stood on the bank of the river. Suddenly seven cows came up out of the river, fine looking and fat; and they fed in the meadow. Then behold, seven other cows came up after them, poor and very ugly and gaunt, such ugliness as I have never seen in all the land of Egypt. And the gaunt and ugly cows ate up the first seven, the fat cows. When they had eaten them up, no one would have known that they had eaten them, for they were just as ugly as at the beginning.

So I awoke. Also I saw in my dream, and suddenly seven heads came up on one stalk, full and good. Then behold seven heads, withered, thin, and blighted by the east wind, sprang up after them. And the thin heads devoured the seven good heads. So I told this to the magicians, but there was no one who could explain it to me." Then Joseph said to Pharaoh, "The dreams of Pharaoh are one; God has shown Pharaoh what He is about to do: The seven good cows are seven years, and the seven good heads are seven years; the dreams are one. And the seven thin and ugly cows which came up after them are seven years, and the seven empty heads blighted by the east wind are seven years of famine. This is the thing which I have spoken to Pharaoh. God has shown Pharaoh what He is about to do. Indeed seven years of great plenty will come throughout all the land of Egypt; but after them seven years of famine will arise, and all the plenty will be forgotten in the land of Egypt; and the famine will deplete the land. So the plenty will not be known in the land because of the famine following, for it will be very severe. And the dream was repeated to Pharaoh twice because the thing is established by God, and God will shortly bring it to pass. "Now therefore, let Pharaoh select a discerning and wise man, and set him over the land of Egypt. Let Pharaoh do this, and let him appoint officers over the land, to collect one-fifth of the produce of the land of Egypt in the seven plentiful years. And let them gather all the food of those good years that are coming, and store up grain under the authority of Pharaoh, and let them keep food in the cities. Then that food shall be as a reserve for the land for the seven years

of famine which shall be in the land of Egypt that the
land may not perish during the famine."

—Genesis 41:14-36

This chapter commenced the beginning of God's invisible hand now showing forth to Joseph in favour from the king. I can hear Joseph saying, "This is the Lord's doing, and it is marvellous in my eyes." The Bible recorded that Pharaoh gave an order to release Joseph from the captivity that Potiphar and his wife had kept him in unjustly. I see and I declare your release from the captivity that people, life challenges have kept you, in Jesus name.

Let us consider this for a second: all this happened suddenly and without any notice given to Joseph that he would be freed that day. I can imagine Joseph going to bed the previous night, and just like on every past day in the prison, he looked forward to the regular old prison duties the following morning. As usual, Joseph attended to his regular prison rota for the following day and made all necessary plans to execute them in the morning; however, when he woke up the following morning, something new happened. He was free to go, and he was needed by the king in the palace very urgently too. The Bible said not only was he brought quickly out of the dungeon but he was also shaved, dressed up to reflect the presence of royalty, and then brought into the palace.

I can imagine Joseph asking, *what is going on? Is this for real? How does the king know that I am here?* These and many more questions flashed through the mind of Joseph. Given that the chief butler had forgotten him for two full years; it eluded him who his benefactor could be.

Listen to me. God's plan for your life will soon come to fruitfulness and suddenly too; it will all be like a dream, and a good one at that. One minute, Joseph was in a very dirty prison, wearing the prison rag, and another minute, he was in the palace, right in the presence of the king, dressed in golden clothing; what a surprising moment. I prophesy to you, in the name of the Lord Jesus, that your moment has come to be celebrated.

Very important, readers—Joseph was not carried away with the new attentions from the throne, and he retained his connectivity with God and was coolheaded with what was coming ahead of him. He knew that for the king to request for him, there must be a reason for the call, and if he must get his freedom, he must satisfy the king's need; hence, he was prepared though unsure as to the reason for the king's call (Proverbs 22:29).

Joseph's curiosity and skillfulness were soon put to test when he arrived before the king. The dreams of the king were shared with him, and the king was eager for interpretation; Joseph's abilities and skills were tested. The king commended Joseph's ability and gift to interpret dreams, but rather than Joseph taking the glory that belonged to God, he directed all honour and glory to the Lord.

In verse 16, Joseph said that it was not him but God who was the one that would give answer of peace to the pharaoh.

Children of God, when heaven eventually opens your door of greatness, ensure that you do not showcase yourself and accord to yourself the glory, honour, and fame that belong to God, for God will not share his glory with anyone.

Now that Joseph has given the glory unto whose it should be in the presence of Pharaoh, the heavenly Father, therefore, has a duty to continue to glorify himself. Consequently, God gave the interpretations of the dreams of Pharaoh unto Joseph who, in turn, delivered it unto the king. Oh yes, Joseph stood the test before Pharaoh, and he delivered.

But you must understand, my friend that it took God many years of preparation at different levels of challenges and stages to get Joseph ready to stand before the king. Equally, you must understand that all the challenges that you are going through are the stages through which God is getting you ready for your future wealth. So ensure that you learn everything that God wants you to learn in the season of trials, and let patience fully have its perfect work in you so that you lack nothing. Your day of celebration shall surely come, so be ready.

Joseph did not only interpret the dreams of the king, but by the enabling power of God, he was also able, in God's wisdom, to provide clear directions not only unto the king but also for the country of Egypt and also save the world.

Proverbs 22:29 says that any man that is skillful in what he does shall stand before the king. Ensure that you are skillful in whatsoever you do so that when you come face-to-face with your king or pharaoh, you will lack nothing. It may be further education that someone needs, and it may be the acquiring of new skills that are needed, but whatsoever you must have or update on, please ensure that you have them; you must not meet the king or pharaoh unprepared.

Chapter 17

The Dreamer and the Wealthy Place

And the thing was good in the eyes of Pharaoh, and in the eyes of all his servants. And Pharaoh said unto his servants, Can we find such a one as this is, a man in whom the Spirit of God is? And Pharaoh said unto Joseph, Forasmuch as God hath shewed thee all this, there is none so discreet and wise as thou art: Thou shalt be over my house, and according unto thy word shall all my people be ruled: only in the throne will I be greater than thou. And Pharaoh said unto Joseph, See, I have set thee over all the land of Egypt. And Pharaoh took off his ring from his hand, and put it upon Joseph's hand, and arrayed him in vestures of fine linen, and put a gold chain about his neck; And he made him to ride in the second chariot which he had; and they cried before him, Bow the knee: and he made him ruler over all the land of Egypt. And Pharaoh said unto Joseph, I am Pharaoh, and without thee shall no man lift up his hand or foot in all the land of Egypt.

—Genesis 41:37-44

When Joseph got before Pharaoh, all of a sudden, it dawned on Joseph that his time and season had finally come, particularly, when, according to verse 37 above, the interpretation and counsel of Joseph (once a prisoner, a slave, and a foreigner) were pleasing unto Pharaoh and his servants.

Listen to me, sons of God, when you enter into your time and season, you will discover that every suggestion you give will be acceptable at all corners. When you bid for a business tender, your quote will be the most suitable. When you apply for a good-paying job, irrespective of how badly you think that you have performed at the interview, you will still get the job because your time and season have come and your chances are set for the taking. Ecclesiastes 9:11.

The Bible recorded that, as a result of the godly advice that Joseph gave to the king, they acknowledged that the Spirit of God dwelt in him. How come? All because Joseph had lifted God up before Pharaoh as the only one that could provide answers to his challenges; and since God was lifted up, he, in return, drew men (Pharaoh and his servants) unto himself. Do you know that if you continue to lift Christ up and pass the glory unto him as he brings you into your time, season, and chance, God will continue to draw unto himself all men that he wishes to draw?

As a consequence of Joseph lifting God up before Pharaoh and Pharaoh seeing God inside of Joseph, Pharaoh had no other option but to tap into the wisdom of God that was loaded right inside of Joseph. The Bible recorded that Pharaoh made Joseph the prime minister of the whole Egyptian nation. Not only that but he also gave him the absolute power over every Egyptian—this also included his former masters, Potiphar and his wife.

Hear the words of the king or pharaoh of Egypt in Genesis 41:40 and 41: *"Thou shalt be over my house, and according unto thy word shall all my people be ruled: only in the throne will I be greater than thou. See, I have set thee over all the land of Egypt."* All because Joseph paid the prices of the processes that now qualified him before God—to receive God's knowledge, understanding, and wisdom to interpret God's revelations as thrown by God unto Pharaoh in his dreams.

Beloved, please ensure that you also pay your prices of the processes that you may go through in the form of trials and challenges, for when the challenges and trials are eventually over and patience has done its full work in you, you will, therefore, lack nothing, and then you shall be lifted into your wealthy place (Psalms 66:10-12).

It was now very clear to Potiphar that this was for real. Not only had Joseph been released from the king's prison, but he was also now the best friend of the king and the prime minister of Egypt. A stranger, become the prime minister of the first civilised nation of the world—who voted for him? How did he do it? Who did he know? Were these the questions in the mouth of Potiphar and all his associates? May the Lord surprise all your adversaries by your sudden promotion.

But the sudden bond that now existed between Joseph and Pharaoh was not fixed by any human hand; instead, it was induced and orchestrated by the heavenly God that, according to the book of Daniel 4:25 and 31, confirmed that he ruleth in the kingdom of men and giveth it only to those he choseth.

The bond that God put between Joseph and Pharaoh was so tight to the point that Pharaoh did the impossible, which he had never done for any of his officials before. The Bible recorded that Pharaoh took off his ring from his hand and put it on Joseph's hand (this represented handing over his majestic authority to Joseph). Joseph was given the "power of attorney" to act on behalf of the king in all matters of government.

The king also arrayed him in vestures of fine linen, put a gold chain about his neck, seated him in the second chariot of the king, caused all men (even Potiphar's entire household) to bow to Joseph, and finally, made him to rule over everything that existed in Egypt.

Remember that Joseph had not made it through into this position of honour by his efforts or by working hard; in fact, Joseph, in every way, was disqualified for the race of leadership in Egypt. The "curriculum vitae" of Joseph is as follows: a foreigner in the land of Egypt and a foreigner to the culture and civilisation of Egypt; brought into Egypt in chains and sold into slavery; served as Potiphar's slave for many years, accused of attempted rape, and convicted as a criminal and a jailbird; a dreamer endowed with the gift of interpretation of dreams; and now the prime minister of the first civilized and most powerful nation of the world. May this be your story soon, my friend, in Jesus name.

You may ask why I took the time to enumerate Joseph's circumstances in that detailed manner above. The answer is straightforward: it is to show to you that your past mistakes do not matter when God is ready to get involved in your matters; your failure too is irrelevant, and neither are any negative labels or judgments that men have placed on you. I heard you say, "I was falsely accused and sent down to prison." That too will work together for your good, providing that you love God and are called according to his purpose.

CHAPTER 18

The Fulfilment of His Dream

*And the seven years of plenteousness that was in the land
of Egypt were ended. And the seven years of dearth began
to come, according as Joseph had said: and the dearth was
in all lands; but in all the land of Egypt there was bread.
And when all the land of Egypt was famished, the people
cried to Pharaoh for bread: and Pharaoh said unto all the
Egyptians, Go unto Joseph; what he saith to you, do. And
the famine was over all the face of the earth: and Joseph
opened all the storehouses, and sold unto the Egyptians;
and the famine waxed sore in the land of Egypt. And
all countries came into Egypt to Joseph for to buy corn;
because that the famine was so sore in all lands.*

—Genesis 41:53-57

*And when Joseph came home, they brought him the
present which was in their hand into the house, and
bowed themselves to him to the earth.*

—Genesis 43:26

This chapter is so beautiful—both to write and to read, I hope—because it brings home to all that it does not matter how long you have been waiting for the promises of God in your life, and it does not matter how long it takes for your God-given dream to be actualized. What is important is that a set and God's appointed day will come when the dream, his dream inside of you, will come to fulfillment, providing that you have been in the perfect will of God.

Following the passage of the season of plenty, Joseph, a man filled with God's wisdom to execute God's agenda, has stored much food for the days ahead when there will be famine in the nations of the earth. You will think that God has done this to protect the Egyptians, but I will submit to you that God has, in his mind, a great plan of provision for the human race and, most importantly, for the household of Israel; hence, he sent Joseph into the most civilized country to put things in place even though they did not know him fully (Psalms 105:17-19).

Equally, my brethren, when God's dream comes to actualization, you must know that you are just a part of the story and you are not the story itself, for the story continues.

The actualization of Joseph occurred in stages: firstly, it was freedom from human and system limitation; secondly, it was unprecedented promotion in the land of a total stranger; thirdly, it was favour that brought him into the corridor of the king and made him the mover and shaker in Egypt; and lastly, he witnessed the days when his family bowed down to him in service, just as he said to them about his dreams many years ago.

Just like God did in the case of Joseph, it is good to understand that our God always works in stages, and he will continue to work until completion is actualized, even until the coming of the Lord Jesus Christ. Philippians 1:6.

All of a sudden, the slave boy, subjected to prison for no crime, had now become the household name. The Bible established that when famine came to town, when the Egyptians went to the royal—as it was supposed to be, originally, before God interrupted the flow of authority in Egypt—the king referred them to Joseph, in Genesis 41:55.

What the king was saying, knowingly or unknowingly, was that "Guys, time has changed, I am no longer in charge of the affairs of Egypt, I am just a ceremonial head, what makes one live or die (food) is now in the hands of Joseph, and if you want to live and not die of hunger, do whatsoever Joseph tells you to do, and that also applies to you, Potiphar."

I declare into your life as a prophet of the living God: may the good Lord of mercy that overruled the judgment of Potiphar with his mercy—James 2:13, prevail in his mercy over all judgment of your enemy, may he cause the helper of your destiny to locate you and bring you out of every prison and challenge of life where you have been hidden and constrained, may he send favour and unmerited grace to bring you into your God-appointed palace, may he empower you to a degree of relevance, may he declare and announce you so that people may celebrate you, and may he lay a table of great feast for you in the presence of your enemies, in the name of the Lord Jesus Christ.

But remember, all this happened suddenly, after everything Joseph had been through for many years, and from one challenge into another, throughout the situations, he was calm and cool and continued to trust in God and worship him. Can you, please, be another Joseph, can you trust God in his word, and can you just be resolute in faith and continue to expect the God of suddenness? It was still surprising that even to the last moment before the king called for Joseph, God never revealed to him His next move, but Joseph resolved to trusting God, he continued to be on the side of God, irrespective of where he was kept. What about you?

Now that God has done the impossible, now that God has interrupted the political, constitutional, and legal system of a civilized country such as Egypt in order to plant his elect in the highest political and economical position of the land—I mean, now that the ruler in the kingdom of men—Daniel 4:25 and 31, has relegated and demoted Pharaoh to a mere ceremonial head and rested real power in his dream carrier by the name Joseph—God moved to phase two of his plan, which was to bring the brothers and family of Joseph to Egypt to bow to him and serve him.

I see relocation on your way, I see heaven repositioning you into a position of authority, and I see you holding an economical and political position, even in a land where you have been rejected. I see God creating your space, and if there is no room for creation, I see God rearranging the top so that you can occupy your space, in Jesus name. Say a bigger *amen*.

The Bible said in verse 56 that there was famine all over the face of the earth. God that knew tomorrow and that knew what lay in the future ensured that Joseph was well positioned at the peak of life itself so that every nation of the world would come over to him to get their daily supplies; indeed, God made a slave/life-sentenced prisoner to become the head of government of the most civilized economy of the world, with no citizenship, no formal education, and no democratic majority vote, but notwithstanding, the counsel of the Lord stood.

Joseph, because of his new location and position, became popular overnight to the point whereby people all over the world began to troop in to him for their survival. Joseph, all of a sudden, became the most important guy in the then universe, all because he paid his dues and allowed the due processes as God allowed and permitted it to complete, and now, the result was envious. Readers, please let patience and endurance have their full work in you so that you may lack nothing, and ensure that you (not God but you) humble yourself under the mighty hand of the Most High God, and at his appointed time, he will lift you up.

The dream of Joseph came to the climax when his brothers came to Egypt to purchase food. Genesis 42:8 confirmed that Joseph's brothers did not know him, but I would rather put it differently—the brothers of Joseph did not recognize him because they were not expecting him to be in Egypt, talked much of being the ruling authority in the land. Remember, they sold him to the Ishmaelites, and because enemies always think in a straight line—just as their master Satan thought in a straight line that if he could hang Jesus Christ on the cross, then the hand of death would catch up with him, and once Jesus Christ is dead, then God had lost. But Satan never knew that all things worked together for good when God is involved. Note this, what ever 'straight line' negative plans of your enemy towards you, given that God is aware, it will work for your good in Jesus name.

Listen to me, readers, does the straight-line journey that your enemies had sold you into, really matter? Not at all. As far as God is concerned, it always leads to his planned wealthy place. Psalm 66:10-12.

Whether or not they recognize him is not the issue; the relevant and practical position of things now is that they need food to survive, or else, they will die, and the only source of their provision is in Egypt, and to get the food in Egypt, they must show respect to the lords of the land. Unknown to them, Joseph was the super lord, and they must recognize him as such. Son of God, your negative and degrading past records don't matter; once God restores you into your wealthy place, everyone will adjust immediately. May the good Lord lift you up, in Jesus name!

Genesis 42:8 said that Joseph knew his brothers and that Joseph remembered his dreams that he had in the time past, and right in his very face and eyes, as the Lord promised, the dream of Joseph came to actualization. May all dreams of God inside of you come to fulfillment. In verse 13 of the same chapter, the brothers of Joseph addressed him as "my lord" and referred to themselves as his servants. In Genesis 43:26, the Bible said that Joseph's brothers prostrated for him in his house.

Also, in Genesis 44:7-10, 13-14, 19-22, 27, and 30-33, it was recorded that Joseph's brothers referred to him as lord and, with their own mouths, made themselves his subjects; indeed, the counsel of the Lord had come to pass, and God's dreams, as revealed to Joseph, had come to pass in spite of all challenges and oppositions. May the God that did it for Joseph bring to pass all his dreams that have been deposited inside of you, in the name of his son, Jesus Christ. Amen.

The last revelation I will like to draw out here is in the attitude of Joseph towards his brothers now that God has fulfilled his dreams. Now that power has changed hands, one will expect Joseph to play a revengeful match and make his brothers pay dearly for all the pains they have caused him, but rather than take the position of God and seek revenge, Joseph forgave his brothers wholeheartedly because of the scope of knowledge that he had acquired during his challenging times.

Remember that no matter your current challenge, it cannot be worse than this, and it can only get better. Also remember that if you cannot stand the heat of trials and challenges, then you are not ready for your season of success. Always see God in your trials and challenges, and you shall always enter into his rest, just like Joseph.

Joseph, after coming out of the traumatic situations that he had been through, was able to sum it up in one sentence in the book of Genesis 50:20: *"You meant it for evil but the Lord used it for my good."* He forgave his brothers from the depth of his heart. Please forgive all that brought you into this difficult situation, and please forgive wholeheartedly now that you are through from all the hard times they have put you through. Remember that all things have worked out for your good because you love God and you are called according to God's purpose.

To every reader of mine that is still going through hard, difficult, and challenging times brought on you by close ones, family members, or someone you really trust, one of your keys out of this situation is forgiveness, and just as Joseph, say in your heart, "I forgive you, yes, you meant it for evil for me, but God will use it for my good," and may it be unto you, just as you believe and confess, in Jesus name. Amen.

Word from the Author

I hope that the Lord has blessed you in the reading of this treasure book. It may be the case that you are led to call or write, either you want to inform me that you have now committed your life unto the Lord Jesus Christ and become part of God's family, or you wish to share your testimony with me of how this book has been a blessing to you; maybe you need a prayer of agreement or wish to invite me to your churches' ministries and conferences to preach, teach, and minister to God's people.

Please make use of the contact information stated below:

dr.martins@csbci.org.uk or prophet@martinsbatireministries.org

I look forward to hearing and reading from you.

If you are within reach of our fellowship center, please join us in our power-packed services. You can also join us *live* from anywhere in the world every Sunday via You Tube streaming; for further information of how to log in via You Tube and for the timing of our Sunday Worship Services and Tuesday evenings

Bible Study and Prayer Services or any other information, visit www.csbci.org.uk.

Remember this: you are a spirit, you live in the body, and you have a soul. So continue to nourish your spirit man, continue to develop your soul in the word of God, and be conformed in your body to become the temple wherein God can dwell forever.

Watch out for my next book, and may the Lord bless you richly. Shalom. Shalom.

Prophet Dr. Martins Batire
PhD (USA), Solicitor (Non Practicing UK), LLM (Lond), PG.Dip (Law), LLB (Hons)

General Overseer
Christ Miracle Evangelical Ministries International
Christ Shalom Bible Center

and

The President
Martins Batire Ministries (MBM)